Blessings, Curses, Hopes, and Fears

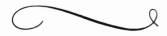

Blessings, Curses, Hopes, and Fears

Psycho-Ostensive Expressions
In Yiddish

JAMES A. MATISOFF

A Publication of the
Institute for the Study of Human Issues
Philadelphia

Manufactured in the United States of America

Library of Congress Cataloging in Publication Data:

Matisoff, James A
    Blessings, curses, hopes, and fears.

    Bibliography: p.
    1. Yiddish language—Terms and phrases. 2. Proverbs, Yiddish. 3. Blessing and cursing. I. Title.
PJ5118.M3   437′.9′47   79–10813
ISBN 0–915980–94–0

For information, write:

Director of Publications
ISHI
3401 Science Center
Philadelphia, Pennsylvania 19104
U.S.A.

to the memory of Uriel Weinreich,
zikhroyne livrokhe

and to my parents,
zoln zey lebn un zayn gezúnt

TABLE OF CONTENTS

field linguistics, anthropology, ethnography, folklore;
sociolinguistics; psychosemantics, psychology, psychotherapy

NOTES [pp. 95-133]

BIBLIOGRAPHY [pp. 134-140]

ACKNOWLEDGMENTS

It is a great pleasure to thank the friends, colleagues, students, and relatives (not mutually exclusive categories!) who have been kind enough to give me their comments, criticisms, addenda, and corrections over the years that this manuscript has been gestating. The book is much stronger because of their help, though of course I alone am to blame for any inadequacies or errors which remain. I especially want to thank Reinhold A. Aman, Robert Austerlitz, Paul K. Benedict, Ariel Bloch, Chana Bloch, Baruch Bokser, Wallace L. Chafe, Irene Eber, Murray B. Emeneau, Charles Fillmore, Marvin I. Herzog, Benjamin Hrushovski, Zelda Kahan, Terrence S. Kaufman, Edward H. Kimball, Paul Kiparsky, Barbara Kirshenblatt-Gimblett, Robert Kirsner, William Labov, Charlotte Linde, Jacob Lubliner, Yakov Malkiel, Joseph Malone, Bernice Matisoff, Maurice Matisoff, Susan Matisoff, Dov Noy, Piyale Cömert Öztek, Herbert Paper, Miriam Petruck, Mordkhe Schaechter, Martin Schwartz, Dan I. Slobin, Norval Slobin, Leonard Talmy, Deborah Tannen, Benji Wald, Beatrice Weinreich, Max Weinreich, and Karl E. Zimmer.

Mikhl Herzog gave generously of his time to correct the first manuscript version of 1972, which had a number of transcriptional inconsistencies, dialecticisms, and errors of fact. Joe Malone, by providing me with Irish parallels to many of the Yiddish expressions discussed, first opened my eyes to the possibilities of extending this sort of investigation to other languages. Paul Kiparsky, in a long and sensitive letter, defended generative grammar against some of the charges I made in the Introduction, while confessing his own malaise at all the 'aspects of language' that the generative approach has been unable to illuminate.

To Benjamin Hrushovski, whose enthusiasm was responsible for the first published version of this study -- in Hebrew -- go my special thanks. To the gifted translator, Chana Kaufman Kronfeld, *a kush in yeder éyverl.* Thanks also to the editor of *Ha-sifrut,* Gideon Toury, who managed to sandwich the editorial work on the Hebrew manuscript between tours of duty in the Israeli armed forces.

To Rey Aman, who revealed to me the true vastness of the field of verbal abuse studies, my thanks and best wishes for the success of his journal *(Maledicta)* and monograph series.

To my typists, Mary Erbaugh (1973 version) and David Magier (final camera-ready version), what can I say? This book would not have been possible without their heroic efforts.

Finally, to the directors and staff of ISHI, especially David A. Feingold, Betty and Joel Jutkowitz, and Douglas Gordon, my enduring gratitude. Seeing this work published at last is a little like marrying off a beloved but aging daughter.

FOREWORD

This book is amateurish in all senses of the word. Firstly because its subject matter is far removed from my area of professional competence -- Southeast Asian linguistics. But secondly because it is written out of love.

The first version of this study, called "Psycho-ostensive expressions in Yiddish," was produced in March-April 1972, and circulated in manuscript form to a number of colleagues and close friends. There was a startling flood of response, most of it encouraging. People sent me additional or variant examples from Yiddish, and parallel examples from other languages. A number of errors of fact were caught, transcriptional inconsistencies noted. Best of all, the whole approach -- informal, interdisciplinary -- seems to have struck a chord.

The revised version, incorporating all the corrections and as many of the additions as I could, was prepared in May 1973, and circulated in mimeographed form (118 pages) that summer. It is substantially identical to what the reader now holds in his hands. In the years since then, there has been a steady trickle of interest in this study and requests for copies still come in. (Some 200 copies have now been distributed in this 'underground' way.)

Feeling well compensated by all this positive feedback, I did not care too much at first if *Psycho* (as I always referred to it in my own mind) ever actually got published. Various attempts were made to submit it to journals or collections of articles, but it was deemed too long and/or not scholarly enough for those media.

In 1973-74, Professor Benjamin Hrushovski of Tel Aviv University came to Berkeley to lecture on linguistically oriented literary criticism. I happened to show him *Psycho*, and he speedily arranged to have it translated into Hebrew and published in its entirety in *Ha-sifrut*, a Tel Aviv journal devoted to the theory of literary criticism and comparative literature (December 1974). The translation, by Chana Kaufman Kronfeld, was excellent and imaginative, and there is now at last a way of saying *allo-malo-petitive* in Hebrew.

The next chapter of this odyssey involves Reinhold A. Aman, an academic rebel and energumen who has founded an international society called Maledicta, devoted to the scientific study of verbal aggression and abuse. Although cursing is only one of the types of speech act discussed in *Psycho*, Aman planned to publish it in his Maledicta Monograph Series. This has not turned out to be possible, though a brief summary did appear in the first issue of the journal *Maledicta* (1977) under the title 'Malediction and psycho-semantic theory.'

Now finally this work has found its ultimate home as an ISHI Publication -- which seems highly appropriate, since ISHI's expanding program in linguistics has made room both for Yiddish and for Southeast Asian languages.

I suppose that my interest in formulas, set expressions, collocations, proverbs, and the like is somehow connected to a deepseated need for security -- the comfortable feeling that one is saying exactly the right thing under a particular set of circumstances. Unlike most Americans, who as Zimmer (1958) and Tannen and Öztek (1977) point out, seem to be rather ashamed of formulaic expressions, feeling that they should come up with something 'original' on special occasions (e.g. funerals), I have always liked the pontifical thunk that a resounding well-placed cliché can make in the middle of a conversation. In fact, one of my (former) friends once publicly called me a 'duck-billed platitude.'

Because the subject of this book is relevant to so many different disciplines, it is understandable that its approach might appear superficial to somebody who is committed to a particular academic specialty, or who has a specific theoretical position to defend. This book has already been read by a highly diverse group of people: Yiddishists, folklorists, sociolinguists, literary critics, anthropologists, 'lexical semanticists,' ethnopsychiatrists, discourse ana-

lysts (as well as by general linguists, and just plain folks). There
is no way that any outsider can satisfy professional standards in all
of these disciplines at once. (I myself would be quite skeptical if
some Yiddish scholar were to start involving himself in Proto-Tibeto-
Burman reconstruction.) What is surprising and gratifying to me,
however, is that scholars in all these fields, despite any reserva-
tions they might have, or changes in emphasis or terminology they
might like to see, have at least been stimulated to react to this
book. Many have declared it to be useful to their thinking, or to
fit right in with some aspect of a problem they had already been
working on from another viewpoint.

At this point it might be appropriate to say a few words about
the personal and intellectual background of this book.

Though I am certainly not a native speaker of Yiddish, I was
exposed to the language rather more than most American Jewish children
of my generation. My father was born in White Russia near Minsk in
1910, and grew up speaking only the local subdialect of 'Litvish' or
Northeastern Yiddish until his arrival in the U.S. in 1923. My mother
was born in New York City, but her parents were both Yiddish-English
bilinguals, and she acquired a solid knowledge of the language from
childhood. By the time I was born in 1937, my parents' Yiddish had
become heavily influenced by English. Although this seriously inter-
fered with its purity, it did make it easier to understand. Further
motivations for learning Yiddish were to understand my essentially
monolingual paternal grandparents, and to figure out what my parents
were saying when they tried to use Yiddish as an adult secret language.

My Yiddish received a severe blow when I studied German, and did
not recover until I began teaching at Columbia in 1966. There I was
exposed for the first time to the world of Yiddish scholarship, and
to the use of the purest form of the language for literary and
scholarly purposes, thanks to the brilliant ambiance created by the
work of Uriel Weinreich, carried on at Columbia after his untimely

death by Marvin I. Herzog and Mordkhe Schaechter. In 1968 and 1969,
Schaechter and I taught together in the Weinreich Memorial Yiddish
Language Summer Program at Columbia. By this time my increased
command of Yiddish had ruined my German again.

Although I could hardly escape the influence of generative grammar, my graduate training at Berkeley (1962-64) had infused me
with a healthy respect for data and an eclectic, heuristic approach to
linguistic theory.[i] Since I returned to Berkeley as a faculty member
in 1970, this tolerant attitude has been reinforced by the intellectual diversity of my colleagues.

So one day in 1972, as I was sitting around at home feeling
eclectic, and having nothing urgent of a Southeast Asian nature on
my mind, somebody must have sneezed. As the automatic *Tsu gezúnt!*
rose allo-bono-petitively to my lips, the idea for this study was
born. (It would be immodest to compare that sneeze to the apple that
fell on Newton's head -- *nisht tsúgeglikhn* ["not to be compared"],
as we say.)

My data base included material of several sorts. First of all,
introspectional data derived from using myself as an informant. This
was admittedly a tricky business given my less-than-native intuitions,
but all introspectional examples have since been checked both for
grammatical accuracy and pragmatic appropriateness, by fully native
speakers. Secondly, elicited data from informants of all sorts,
starting with my mother (who, bless her, took the time to write me a
ten-page letter in tiny handwriting, packed with psycho-ostensive expressions). As indicated above, many additional examples were later
provided by friends and colleagues reacting to the two manuscript
versions. Thirdly, as a source of written examples, I decided to use
as my corpus the superlative collections of Yiddish jokes and anecdotes
compiled by Immanuel Olsvanger, *Röyte Pomerantsen* (1947) and *L'Chayim*
(1949). These are written in a fully natural and flavorful style,
with an uncanny accuracy in reproducing the rhythms of fluent everyday
speech.[ii] Psycho-ostensives abound on every page and occur in well-
defined, richly elaborated situational contexts. (The genre of joke-

telling requires that a scene be set with precision!) I let these
data flow over me, with no theoretical *parti pris*, and soon the most
useful categorial apparatus for classifying and organizing them
seemed to emerge spontaneously. The categories *recognitive / petitive / fugitive, bono- / malo-,* and *auto- / allo-* [*below, section
2.0*] are no doubt ridiculously simple -- 'pseudo-semantic,' one un-
charitable soul has called them -- but they happen to work very
nicely. As my data base has expanded over the years, it has not
proven necessary to change that conceptual framework in order to
accommodate the new facts.

That is more than one can say for linguistic theory in general
during the past several years.

The Introduction [*section 1.0*], where I place this book in the
context of the American linguistic scene as a whole, has (purposely)
not been rewritten at all since 1973, and may therefore appear rather
dated. But to coin a phrase, *There is nothing new under the sun.*
Blessings, curses, oaths, congratulations, etc., are all *speech acts*
-- though I had never heard of that now so fashionable term when I
wrote the body of this book. The psycho-ostensives can only be pro-
perly understood in the context of the entire linguistic and extra-
linguistic (psychological, situational) environments in which they
appear. Although this point is made throughout the book, I never used
the now popular terms *discourse analysis* or *pragmatics.*

But maybe like Molière's Monsieur Jourdain, I was talking prose
all along without realizing it![iii]

A word about the style in which this book is written. Most
people appear to like the way I write, finding my style, despite its
obvious imperfections, to be something of a relief from the dreariness
of the usual sort of academic writing. As always, however, one can't
please everybody. I have been accused of irreverence and flippancy
on the one hand, and of cuteness and mawkishness on the other. Some
are freaked out by my mixture of stylistic levels, my penchant for
juxtaposing colloquialisms and learnèd locutions in the same sentence.
To this I can only reply that I can't help it.

More disturbing is the implication that the content of this book is superficial because it is written in a clear and simple way. A well-known sociolinguist of the older generation, while conceding that my terminology is 'resourceful and likely to prove very useful cross-culturally,'[iv] feels that I have 'refused to analyze the material linguistically,' and that it is 'a regression to only list it and give running commentary.' What can I say? I would only beg the reader not to confuse simplicity with simple-mindedness -- any more than he would confuse obscurity with profundity.

As my final platitude, I would like to close with the observation that *one man's meat is another man's poison*. To those who do manage to find some intellectual nourishment in these pages, let me say, from the bottom of my heart, *Eat it in good health!*

J.A.M.

Berkeley, California

NOTES

[i]My theoretical views are presented in some detail (though rather polemically) in the Introduction to The Grammar of Lahu (1973), pp. *xliv* - *li*.

[ii]Olsvanger was a serious scholar and litterateur who polished and re-worked the style of his anecdotes over a period of thirty years. His first collections were published in 1921 and 1935 (see Bibliography), and these already contained the bulk of the material he presented in 1947 and 1949. His material in its final form is clearly meant to be read aloud to an appreciative audience.

*iii*My colleague, Karl Zimmer, *a gezúnt tsu im*, has gone so far as to call me a *nachträglicher Bahnbrecher*, or 'belated trailblazer.' Of course he is one himself! Back in 1958, as a graduate student, he wrote a term paper on 'Situational formulas' that already raised many of the issues treated in this study. I was unaware of this unpublished paper until 1976.

*iv*For an illustration of how the conceptual framework outlined in this book may be applied to other languages, see the paper by Tannen and Öztek on Greek and Turkish formulaic expressions (1977), which inspired much of the Epilogue of this book [*section 12.0 below*].

LIST OF ABBREVIATIONS

<	is derived from (in etymologies)
app.	appendix
dat.	dative case
Deut.	Deuteronomy
dim.	diminutive
Eng.	English
esp.	especially
ex.	example
Fr.	French
gen.	genitive case
Gk	Greek
Gk. App.	Greek Appendix (to Tannen and Öztek 1977)
Heb.	Hebrew
lit.	literally
mod.	modern
NP	noun phrase
pers. comm.	personal communication
RP	*Röyte Pomerantsen* (Olsvanger 1947/1965)
Russ.	Russian
Tk.	Turkish
Tk. App.	Turkish Appendix (to Tannen and Öztek 1977)
ult.	ultimately
Yid.	Yiddish
YP	*Yiddish Proverbs* (Ayalti 1949)

1.0 INTRODUCTION

To say that a language is 'an infinite set of well-formed sentences'[1] is a little like saying that a human being consists of water,
carbon, salt, and trace elements. That is, there are certain restricted contexts in which such statements make sense, even though
there are many other intellectual points of view from which they are
irrelevant and misleading. When we are engrossed in our formalistic
charts and diagrams, writing our rules and playing with our arrows
and brackets, it is easy to forget that we are approaching that mag-
nificent infinite object, Language, in much the same way as the blind
men in the fable approached the elephant.

In particular, most linguists have been operating on the heuristic assumption that the speakers of a language are some kind of
beautifully programmed automata, sentence-generating machines capable
of producing a limitless number of grammatical utterances that conform
in all respects to a fixed set of rules -- the grammar of one's native
language -- that has been internalized in early childhood. This
point of view, as everyone knows, has opened up some brilliantly
successful lines of investigation. But now it is time to move on
from the elephant's cerebral cortex to his primitive brain-stem, his
heart, his gonads, or wherever else the seat of his emotions may be
located.[2]

The work of William Labov and his students has undercut the
overly rigid Chomskyan dichotomy between 'competence' and 'performance' to the point where it is no longer clear in what sense we can
speak of a 'rule of grammar' at all. Variability is now understood
by many to be as basic to linguistic structure as the counter-tendency
toward order and organization. We can easily construct 'an infinite
set of sentences' in any language as to the grammaticality of which
native speakers will violently disagree,[3] each citing his own sacred

1

intuitions as evidence one way or the other. It is precisely this variability which lies at the heart of linguistic creativity.

Language is the frail bridge which we fling across the chasm of the inexpressible and the incommunicable.

Anyone who has ever tried to get any thoughts down on paper knows how hard it is to 'say what you mean.' How much more difficult this is under the time-pressure of ordinary rapid conversation! When we write, we have the leisure to go back and cross things out, add a word here or permute some words there, recast a sentence completely if we have gotten ourselves into a desperate syntactic bind. When we speak, our interlocutors will lose patience with us if we say, 'Just a minute -- I used the perfect tense in that last sentence, but the action referred to really didn't have enough present relevance for that, so I retract it and will use the simple past instead. Also, I'd like to put that adverb at the end of the sentence instead of at the beginning -- I don't know why, it just sounds better.' At this point our listener would be likely to say, 'Go to the devil with your adverbs and your present relevance!', or, if he is a Yiddish speaker, *Gey tsum tayvl mit dayne adverbn un itstike shâyekhdikkayt tsuzamen!*[4]

Under the pressure to communicate rapidly, the edges of the grammar are constantly being bent and deformed, expanded and re-tracted.[5] My daughter's report-card this morning carried the teacher's scrawled comment, *She shuns away from the math area.* How can we be so arrogant as to stigmatize this as a 'performance error?' We might succeed in demonstrating that *shuns away from* derives analog-ically from *shies away from* in some historical sense. But it is not a 'mistake,' for God's sake.[6] It's a rather nice new creation, in fact, and had doubtless already occurred independently in the speech of millions of people of all social classes and degrees of linguistic virtuosity. It already sounds grammatical to me, better and better each time I say it over to myself. The new grammar is constantly being created on top of the willing and yielding ruins of the old. To worry about where 'one' grammar ends and the 'next' grammar begins is a totally meaningless and futile pursuit. Innovations in language are welcomed at least as much as they are resisted.

Everybody knows (but linguists have usually forgotten) that the real communication that goes on during interpersonal exchanges often has very little to do with the actual words that are spoken. We can be talking about the damn cat when all we want to do is go to bed with each other. We can be trading polite commiserations about the weather even as we are thinking how we hate each other, and how gladly we would bathe in the other's blood. From early childhood on, we learn to look for 'the *real* meaning behind the words.' That is, we look for para-linguistic cues to the speaker's real psychic states or attitudes, which his words may be belying. When a parent half-heartedly says, 'That's wonderful, dear,' in response to something the child is showing off to him, the child will understand this as meaning 'Big deal! Go away, kid, you bother me.' When the parent is screaming at the child in sincere fury 'How many times did I tell you[7] not to do that?,' the child knows that it will go far better for him if he says nothing and looks contrite than if he treats the emotional outburst as a real question and answers, 'Well, my best guess is fifteen or sixteen times.' We do not like people who give us a detailed catalogue of their ailments in response to 'How are you?' All that we want from them is a formula, like 'Fine, thank you' or 'Couldn't be better,' or, if they are Yiddish speakers, *Freg nit* ("Don't ask!").

The point is, millions of sentences are 'generated' every day which have a surface structure *and* a deep structure (in the conventional sense) which are totally unrelated to what is really going on in the speaker's (and the listener's) mind. Put another way, any utterance in a language may be associated with an indefinite number of psychic states, and many of these cannot possibly be deduced from the words themselves. If linguists are serious about wanting to integrate meaning into a comprehensive theory of language, these facts must eventually be faced.

Actually there are signs of movement in such a direction. Recent work on the 'presuppositions' underlying utterances[8],

although still largely tied to the generative umbilicus, may yet lead
to the modification of some cherished formalistic attitudes. Consider the sentence, 'He says he will seek legislation distinguishing
marijuana from the more dangerous addictive drugs.'[9] This may be
understood in at least four ways. Either he believes (i.e. 'has a
presupposition that') marijuana is addictive, but not so dangerous as,
say, heroin; or he believes that marijuana is neither very dangerous
nor addictive.[10] On the other hand, he may be quite neutral on the
question of marijuana's danger or addictivity, and may only be seeking
legislation that will enshrine the fact that marijuana is not the
same as other drugs. In this (less likely) interpretation, the two
alternative presuppositions are inside the head of the speaker who is
reporting the legislator's plans, not inside the legislator himself.

Even closer to the concerns of the present paper is the exciting work being done by Wallace L. Chafe,[11] who is beginning to
explore directly the linguistic repercussions of the psychic attitudes (or 'states of consciousness') of the speaker and hearer.

Yiddish has the deserved reputation of being a highly expressive
language. This 'funkiness' has been sentimentalized over with in-
sistent vulgarity by some popular writers.[12] At the other extreme
we find the somewhat solemn academic approach of the professional
Yiddishist, for whom the Yiddish language is primarily the vehicle
for high-minded scholarly endeavor, a precious jewel to be preserved
intact for an ever-dwindling cultural élite.[13] Perhaps the time has
come to stop 'shunning away' from the earthier side of Yiddish, in
the interests of determining just what it is that gives the language
its considerable emotive power.

We shall find that Yiddish has, among its arsenal of expressive
devices, certain well-defined classes of ready-made phrases or
formulas that are typically inserted parenthetically into larger
sentences, and whose only function is to give vent to the speaker's
emotional attitude toward what he is talking about. Each of these
psycho-ostensive expressions is intended by the speaker to be accepted
as the direct linguistic manifestation of his psychic state of the

moment. The speaker wishes to share his emotions explicitly with his
listener, to display them overtly so as to narrow down the possible
range of underlying attitudes which the listener might otherwise guess
to be lurking behind his words. When somebody says,

(i) *Mayn zun, zol er zayn gezúnt un shtark, vet mir dos shikn ahér.*
("My son, *may he be healthy and strong,* will send it here to me."),

he means the listener to make no mistake that he loves his son and
wishes him well.[14] When he says,

(ii) *Góverner Reygn, zol er óysgemekt vern, git mayn zun dem
profesor, a gezúnt tsu im, keyn hesofe nit hayyor.* ("Governor
Reagan, *may he be erased,* isn't giving any raise this year to my
son the professor, *a health to him.*"),

he leaves no doubt about his psychic attitudes toward the various
parties to the action.

      This is not to say that these psycho-ostensive expressions may
not be used mendaciously. Nothing is stopping you from saying,

(iii) *Mayn feter Khaim-Yankl, olevasholem, flegt dos alemól zogn.*
("My Uncle Chaim-Yankl, *upon him peace,* always used to say that."),

when what you really mean is "My uncle, the old cretin, used to give
me that stuff all the time." Often it is not so much that the
speaker is using an emotive formula that actually belies his true
feelings, as that the formula has become a surrogate for the true
feeling, an almost automatic linguistic feature that constant usage
has rendered as predictable and redundant as the concord in number
between subject and verb. The speaker may have no particular feelings one way or the other about old Uncle Chaim-Yankl, but says
olevasholem by pure reflex action. Nevertheless, psycho-ostensives
are often used in Yiddish with utter sincerity, and are very much
a living, breathing part of the language.[15]

      The formation of these emotive expressions is a productive pro-
cess among fully fluent Yiddish speakers, so that it is impossible
to give anything approaching an exhaustive list of them. Virtuosity

in concocting new linguistic variations on the old emotive themes is highly prized. It takes little imagination to say *Tsu gezúnt* ("Gesundheit!") when somebody sneezes. This is indeed a 'ready-made phrase or formula,' about as original as the 'Hello' with which one answers the telephone. But think of the genius of the first person who ever greeted his startled friend's sneeze with:

(iv) *Tsu gezúnt, tsu lebn, tsu lange yor, zolst vaksn un bliyen in der leng un in der breyt vi a Purim-koyletsh!* ("To your health, and life, and longevity, and may you grow and bloom in your length and in your width like a Purim-loaf!")[16]

Jews have always admired articulate, flavorful speech. The Yiddish language provides conventionalized, well-established discourse-slots for the insertion of psycho-ostensive expressions, but there is considerable latitude for individual flights of fancy in filling the slots up.

It is, of course, impossible to predict *a priori* which new variations will catch on, and become adopted by so many speakers that they become 'part of the language' in the sense of 'belonging to the competence of the typical native speaker.' Even more thankless a task would be to try and formulate rigorous 'constraints' on the formation of new psycho-ostensives, in such a way that one could make the negative prediction that a given phrase would never become a standard formula. True, we shall see, for example, that in psycho-ostensive curses one has greater freedom in specifying a particular body-part for the evil to strike than one does in similarly-phrased benedictions [*below, 9.3*]. It sounds better in the abstract to say,

(v) *mayn shver, a krenk zol im aráyn in di yasles...* ("my father-in-law, may a disease enter his gums..."),

than it does to say,

(vi) *mayn tokhter, a gezúnt zol ir aráyn in di yasles...* ("my daughter, may health enter her gums...").

Yet if one's daughter had been suffering from gingivitis, the latter expression would be so appropriate that it would pass unnoticed.

For Jews with limited access to the mainstream of Western culture in the *shtetlekh* of Eastern Europe, the outside Gentile world was often rather hostile, cold, and intimidating. The inner Jewish world, in compensation, despite its material poverty and frequent pettiness, was at least full of overt demonstrations of feeling: heartfelt loves and hatreds, fears and hopes received constant outward expression in the language of the people. It is no accident that Yiddish is sentimentally referred to as *mame-loshn* ("mother-language").

Yiddish psycho-ostensives, despite their richness and variety, all seem to fall into a few large psychosemantic categories, all having to do basically with attitudes toward *good* and *evil*. These include expressions where the speaker is wishing for good things (life, health, prosperity) for himself or his family, or altruistically for people in the out-group; expressions of gratitude for good things received or lamentations for one's troubles; apotropaic locutions used to ward off evil, including expressions that are meant to appease the dead; formulas whereby one calls down evil (death, disease, misfortune) on others; oaths one uses to swear to the truth, sometimes taking the form of wishing evil to oneself in order to convince others of one's veracity.

2.0 SEMANTIC SUBTYPES OF PSYCHO-OSTENSIVE EXPRESSIONS

We shall deal with six basic subtypes of psycho-ostensives. Perhaps that is all there are. All Yiddish psycho-ostensives seem to involve the speaker's attitude toward the good things and the bad things of life. Sometimes this is a passive attitude of acceptance or recognition that good or evil has befallen. At least as often, the speaker assumes a more active psychic stance, expressing his desire, wish, seeking for the good; or conversely, his abhorrence, fear, shunning of the evil; or, perversely, his wish that evil may strike

his fellow man or himself. Perhaps a little home-made nomenclature is
in order here (*pace* any professional psychologists in the audience).*
The relatively passive attitude of acceptance of good or evil we call
recognitive; the (more active) attitude of seeking or desiring we
call *petitive*; and the (more active) attitude of shunning or fearing
we call *fugitive*. Add to these the Greek roots for 'self' and 'other'
(*auto-* and *allo-*), and the Latin roots for 'good' and 'evil' (*bono-*
and *malo-*), and we have all we need for the moment. Thus, e.g., *auto-*
malo-recognitive means 'recognizing that evil has come to oneself;'
allo-bono-petitive means 'wishing for good to come to others,' etc.

These categories, like all others in linguistics, are not mutually exclusive and shade into one another, but they will do as a basis for discussion. As we look at the data, we shall see what syntactic and psychosemantic generalizations can be made, but we will not, God
forbid, distort the data to conform to our theoretical preconceptions.

3.0 BONO-RECOGNITION: THANKS AND CONGRATULATIONS

Let us start on a positive note. Sometimes things do go well in
this world, and the Yiddish speaker feels obliged to acknowledge his
indebtedness to God, from whom all blessings flow, whenever he mentions his own good fortune. One of the most common of these auto-bono-
recognitive expressions is *borkhashém* (< Heb. *barukh ha-shem* "blessed
be the Name [of God]"):

(1) *Ikh bin, borkhashém, gezúnt, un di gesheftn geyen gut.* ("I am,
bless God, healthy, and business is good." RP, p. 44.[17])

(2) *Es geyt, borkhashém, gants gut, un mit der vayb mayner leb ikh
gor fayn.* ("Things are going, bless God, very well, and I'm getting
along fine with my wife." RP, p. 13.)

(3) *Un ikh hob, borkhashém, gehát a sheyn bisl tekhter, hot dos*

---

*Pace is actually a *palliative blessing*, in the sense of pp. 30-31,
below.

gedoyert un gedoyert. ("And I had, bless God, quite a few daughters, so it [marrying them off] took a long, long time." RP,
p. 23.)

(4) *Vos bin ikh? Krank bin ikh? Ikh bin, borkhashém, oyf ale yidn
gezógt gevorn, gezúnt un shtark.* ("What am I? Am I sick? I am,
bless God, may the same be said for all Jews, healthy and strong."
RP, p. 131.)

Already from these few examples we can sense the futility of
trying to set up airtight, mutually exclusive, psycho-semantic categories. While (1) and (2) are relatively pure expressions of the
auto-bono-recognitive attitude,[18] (3) contains something in addition.
The speaker is explaining why he hasn't been able to divorce his
shrewish wife, even though he had desperately been wanting to for the
past fifty years. He had had to marry his daughters off first. Yet
despite this lifelong frustration, he must still thank God for having
given him live, healthy children. Otherwise, if he should let his
underlying resentment towards his children show, God might retaliate
by visiting sickness or death on the children he had been too selfish
to appreciate. God has a way of doing things like that. We see then
that the auto-bono-recognitive formula is here being used in self-
defense, as it were. We must thank God even for mixed blessings in
order to avoid something worse. Our gratitude is really a plea to
be spared further punishment;[19] at some level it is *fugitive* as well
as recognitive.[20]

Sentence (4) is uttered by a rich miser, who has just been
called "sick" by a man who had come to ask him for charity. "What,
me sick?" he is indignantly asking. "I'm as strong as a horse!"
And yet we sense the nervous crossing of fingers that must be going
on in his head. Not only does he use the regular formula *borkhashém,*
but he makes doubly sure of God's good will by using another formula
on top of it, this time a more altruistic allo-bono-petitive one (*oyf
ale yidn gezógt gevorn* "may the same be said for all Jews"). In
his very pride, he is dimly aware of his fundamental helplessness as

a human being. As the proverb has it, *Dem yidns simkhe iz mit a bisl shrek.* ("A Jew's joy has a little fear in it.")[21]

Instead of *borkhashém*, one may use the Germanic-derived expression *Got tsu danken* "thank God" (lit. "[we have] God to thank"):

(5) *Hayyor, Got tsu danken, veln mir nit shtarbn fun hunger.*

("This year, thank God, we won't starve.")

Other possibilities include: *danken Got; a dank Got* (lit. "a thanks [to] God"); *a dank/loyb dem Éybershtn* (lit. "thanks/praise to the Supreme One"); or, with even greater feeling, *a dank un a loyb dir Got* ("thanks and praise to you, God").

Often these formulas of thanks are used by themselves as complete utterances, e.g. in answer to a question concerning one's well-being:

(6a) *Nu, vos makht ir epes?* ("So how are you?")

(6b) *Got tsu danken.* ("Thank God.") / *Borkhashém.*("Bless God.")

We shall be referring to this phenomenon as the *independent use* of psycho-ostensive expressions.[22]

Notice that so far we have been thanking God, and not our fellow-man. Yiddish certainly has expressions available for thanking *people* as well: *a dank* ("Thanks"); *a dank dir/aykh* ("Thank you");[23] *a groysn/sheynem dank (dir/aykh)* ("Thank you very much"),[24] etc. As in English, such phrases may be encapsulated in larger utterances:

(7) *Yo, a dank, efsher vel ikh take nemen nokh a shtíkele.* ("Yes, thanks, maybe I *will* have another teensy piece.")

However, there are certain cultural differences in the occasions when one offers thanks to other people. In English, we thank people for inquiring as to our health (*Fine, thank you*); in Yiddish, if such an inquiry is favored with a straight answer,[25] it is God who usually gets the thanks, not the other person [*see above*]. In English we thank people for compliments (-- *You dance divinely.* -- *Oh, thank you!*). In traditional Yiddish, direct compliments were avoided as much as possible, so as not to provoke the Evil Eye [*below 7.5*].

If one should by mischance be complimented, the usual reaction would certainly not be to thank the complimenter, but rather to mutter some auto-malo-fugitive formula or make a self-deprecatory reply like *Vos redt ir?* ("What are you talking about!").[26]

When true gratitude is to be expressed, as in recognition of a great service done, English uses an emphatic variant of the 'thank you' theme: 'I thank you from the bottom of my heart,' etc. In Yiddish, rather than multiplying such auto-bono-recognitive expressions, one would tend to produce *allo-bono-petitive* ones: i.e. one would *bless* the benefactor rather than thanking him:[27]

(8) *Rebe, lang lebn zolt ir! Ir hot mir gerátevet di tokhter.* ("Oh, rabbi, long may you live! You've saved my daughter!" RP, p. 41.)

The connection between auto-bono-recognition and allo-bono-petition is obvious from the etymology of the standard formula *a ya-sher-koyekh (dir/aykh)* (< Heb. *yiyshar koakh* "may [your] strength be straight"), where one wishes strength for one's benefactor:

(9) *Der balebós ... hot im gefrégt, tsi er vet nit vos esn. Ent-fert der oyrekh: "A groysn yasher-koyekh aykh, esn vel ikh nit..."* ("The householder asked him if he wouldn't eat something. The guest answered, 'More power to you, but I don't feel like eating...' " RP, p. 127.)

Another alternative would be to use a euphemistically negative expression, rather like English 'I don't know how to thank you:' [28]

(10) *Der rov hot genumen dos gelt un hot gezógt mit a groysn zifts: "Oy, keyn dank vel ikh aykh nit zogn!"* ("The rabbi took the money and said with a deep sigh, 'Ah, I won't give you any thanks!' " *L'Chayim,* p. 28.)[29]

One context where Yiddish and English usage closely correspond is in ironically polite expressions of the 'thanks for nothing' variety:

(11) *A sheynem dank aykh, dos iz nit ayer eysek.* ("That's none of your business, thank you.")

(12) *A sheynem dank aykh, mit azoyne inyonim vel ikh shoyn kenen óyskumen eyner aleyn.* ("I can manage such matters very well on my own, thank you.")

If one wishes to be truly insulting while maintaining a spurious attitude of bono-recognition, there is a ready-made put-down available:

(13) *A sheynem dank aykh -- fun a khazer a hor iz oykh epes.* ("Thanks loads -- coming from a pig, even a hair is something.")

Towards God one would never dare to be so brutal. If you are disappointed with what you get, you can always shrug your shoulders and say:

(14) *Nu, Got tsu danken far derfár.* ("Well, thank God for this much.")

To adopt any other attitude would be to expose oneself to divine retaliation for ingratitude [*see below 7.4*]. And besides, who knows how things will turn out in the long run? As the proverb has it:

(15) *Men veyst nit, far vos Got tsu danken.* ("We don't know what to thank God for." YP, p. 92.)

*   *   *

If we call thanking the expression of an underlying *auto*-bono-recognitive attitude, we may regard *congratulations* as reflecting the other-directed counterpart -- i.e. *allo*-bono-recognition. When we congratulate someone, we are giving overt recognition to the fact that he has received one of life's good things.

In Yiddish, congratulatory expressions are not encapsulated parenthetically inside longer sentences, but typically stand alone, in the manner of interjections. The commonest of these is, of course, *mázltov* (< Heb. *mazal tov* "good luck"),[30] which seems to have found its way into general American English. Others in this category include: *zol zayn mit mazl* (lit. "may it be with luck"); *zol zayn mit glik* (*id*.); *a sakh glik* ("lots of luck"); *zol zayn mit fil freyd un glik* (lit. "may it be with much joy and luck"), etc. Thus,

(16) *Ir boyt zikh? Zol zayn mit mazl!* ("You're building yourself [a new house]? I wish you luck!" RP, pp. 91-2.)[31]

(17) *Yánkele, Got hot dir geholfn, zol zayn mit glik! Efsher voltst mir geként layen a finef rubl?* ("Yankele, God has been good to you [lit. "God has helped you"], congratulations! Maybe you could lend me five rubles?" RP, p. 125.)

The key concepts in all these expressions are the words for 'luck', *glik* and *mazl*. Even as one offers congratulations, there is an underlying awareness that nothing is more transitory than good fortune, and that a lifetime of happiness can evaporate in the twinkling of an eye. As the proverbs say:

(18) *Ven Got vil, shist a bezem.* ("If God wills it, [even] a broom can shoot [like a gun]," i.e. "misfortune can always strike from the most unlikely source.")

(19) *Fun glik tsum umglik iz a shpan -- fun umglik tsum glik iz a shtik veg.* ("From fortune to misfortune is but a step -- from misfortune to fortune is a good long way." YP, p. 74.)

The congratulations, therefore, take the form of wishes that the good luck of the beneficiary will continue indefinitely into the future. In our terms, allo-bono-recognition shades into allo-bono-petition [*below, section 6*].

4.0 MALO-RECOGNITION: LAMENTATION AND SYMPATHY

Yiddish is rich in auto-malo-recognitive expressions of the 'woe is me' variety. In fact, one of the commonest of these is the direct cognate of English 'woe is me' -- *vey iz mir* or *vey iz tsu mir:*

(20) *Itst zogt zi, zi vet khásene hobn mit a frantsóyz, vey iz tsu
mir!* ("Now she says she's going to marry a Frenchman, woe is me!")

Other expressions of this type include *a klog tsu mir* (lit. "a lament
to me!"), *a klog tsu mayn velt* (lit. "a lament to my world!"),[32] and
a brokh tsu mir or *a brokh iz mir* (lit. "a breaking [i.e. a cala-
mity] is to me!"). If one wishes to wallow in malo-recognition, one
can string together several of these in a row:

(21) *Farzámt di ban, óngevorn di gesheftn, a brokh, a klog, a
yomer, a gevált!* ("Missed the train, ruined the business deal, what
a calamity, what a debacle, what a kettle of fish, what a crock!"
RP, p. 136.)

A more elaborate and archaic-sounding variant of *vey iz mir* is
az okh un vey tsu mir. *Okh* (cf. German *ach*) almost always occurs in
combination with *vey*, much like English 'alack' in 'alas and alack.'

There is an interesting asymmetry in the psychosemantics of
a klog and *a brokh* on the one hand, and *vey* or *okh un vey* on the
other. As we have seen, when *a klog* and *a brokh* are accompanied
by a first-person dative pronoun, the meaning is always auto-malo-
recognitive. If however, a non-first person pronoun is used, the
meaning is not allo-malo-recognitive (i.e. 'sympathetic') as one would
expect, but rather *allo-malo-petitive:* a curse, a wish that evil may
befall another [*see below, section 9*]. Thus:

(22) *Haynt kumt er oykh nit, a brokh tsu im!* ("He's not coming
today either, a calamity to him!")

(23) *A klog tsu dir, bist meshuge tsi khoser-deye?* ("A lament to
you, are you crazy or just feeble-minded?")

With *vey* or *okh un vey,* however, this shift in attitude does not
accompany the change of pronoun. Non-first person utterances with
these words are expressions of sympathy, not curses:

(24) *Er hot farlorn beyde hent in der milkhome, az okh un vey tsu
im.* ("He lost both his hands in the war, the poor devil.")

(25) *Tate, du lakhst? Az okh un vey tsu dayn gelekhter.* ("You're laughing, father? Woe to your laughter!")[33]

It is often hard to draw the line between a lamentation at one's own sorrow (auto-malo-recognition) and a sympathetic sharing in the sorrow of others (allo-malo-recognition). The more one empathizes with the plight of another, the fuzzier the distinction becomes. Typically one expresses sympathy in Yiddish by auto-malo-recognitives in order to emphasize the genuineness of one's feelings. Nothing is stopping you from using such formulas hypocritically, however, as illustrated by the anecdote about a woman carrying a basket of eggs who has just learned of the death of her friend Sarah:

(26) *"Vos redt ir? Sore iz geshtorbn? Halt nor tsu mayn kôshekl." Un az yene hot genumen ir kôshekl, brekht zi di hent un zogt "A brokh tsu mir!"* (" 'What are you saying? Sore is dead? Hold my basket a minute.' And when the other woman had taken her basket, she wrung her hands and said 'Woe is me!' " RP, p. 44.)[34]

The Yiddish malo-recognitive word *par excellence* is the splendid adverb *nebekh,* whose praises have been sung in the popular literature.[35] This word is usable both in contexts where the speaker is lamenting his own misfortune and in those where he is sympathizing with the misfortune of another:

(27) *Bin ikh nebekh avék fun gvirs shtub on a nedove.* ("So, unfortunate that I am, I left the rich man's house without getting any charity." RP, p. 130.)

(28) *Un der melamed veynt nebekh.* ("And the teacher cried, poor man." RP, p. 125.)

(29) *Er hot zikh nebekh shtark farshémt.* ("He was deeply ashamed, poor man." RP, p. 178.)

(30) *Iz er nebekh gegangen oyf a hîltsernem fus.* ("So he walked around on a wooden leg, poor man." RP, p. 101.)

(31) *A yid a soykher iz a mol geshtanen in krom a gantsn tog, un*

keyn eyn koyne iz nebekh tsu im nit gekumen. ("A Jewish merchant once stood in his store the whole day long, and not a single customer came in, poor man." RP, p. 83.)

(32) *Un di feyglekh fun himl flien avék fun barg in ale kantn, nebekh tseshrókene.* ("And the little birds in the sky flew away from the mountain in all directions, frightened to death, poor things." RP, p. 176.)

(33) *Fregt der tate, nebekh a toyber, "A, vos iz gevorn?"* ("Then the father asked -- he was deaf, poor man -- 'Eh? What happened?' " RP, p. 110.)

(34) *Un bazunders hot fun im gehát tsores der shames fun shul, nebekh a yid a geshvólener oremán.* ("And the one who suffered especially from him was the sexton of the synagogue, who was desperately poor, poor man." RP, p. 129.)[36]

As these examples show, the syntactic properties of *nebekh* are not simple. Sometimes it seems to stand in constituency with the verb of its clause, or what amounts to the same thing, with its clause as a whole (27-31); in other sentences it is more intimately connected to a noun-phrase (32-34).[37] For now we shall content ourselves with mentioning a semantically analogous morpheme that leaps to mind from another language, Lahu, where the verb-particle *šē* may be used to indicate that the speaker finds the action of the clause a cause for regret:

(35) *ɔ-ğâ nû jâ šē lɛ, nâʔ-chɨ̂ qhà-ma tɔ thɔ̂, šɨ e šē ve yɔ̀.* ("His strength was, regrettably, very low, and no matter how much medicine they gave him, he died, regrettably.")[38]

Yiddish speakers are well aware of the humorous potential that psycho-ostensive expressions have when they are used in semantically incongruous contexts. There is a joke about a group of Jewish prisoners being led off to a czarist jail, while a few horrified Jewish women look on. As each prisoner passes the ladies, they ask him what he has been arrested for. The first says that his crime was a passport violation. The women wail and say:

(36) *Oy, nebekh, far a pas!* ("Oh, poor man, for a passport!"
RP, p. 25.)

The second one says that he had tried to evade military service. Like
passport violations, avoidance of military service in the czarist
armies was by no means frowned upon in the Jewish community, and the
women wail again:

(37) *Oy, nebekh, vegn prizív!* ("Oh, poor man, because of military
service!")

The third prisoner goes by, and is asked the same question. He replies
with wry humor:

(38) *Ikh bin nebekh a ganev.* ("I, poor man, am a thief.")

5.0 PETITIVE ATTITUDES

As opposed to recognitive attitudes, where the speaker is simply
acknowledging a good or bad state of affairs, we often encounter
psychic states where the speaker is actively wishing or hoping for
some good or bad eventuality to come to pass. These *petitive* states
may be subclassified according to whether they primarily involve only
the speaker himself (*auto-*), or other people as well (*allo-*); and according to whether it is a good that is wished for (*bono-*) or an evil
(*malo-*).[39] Yiddish has a wealth of devices available for expressing
petitive attitudes. Some of these are so general that they are
usable in all petitive contexts, hostile as well as loving, inner- as
well as outer-directed. Others are restricted to certain subtypes of
petitives.

Among the general petitive structures we may mention the following:

(a) *zoln + Infinitival complement clause.* Along with its many other
uses in Yiddish grammar, the auxiliary verb *zoln* 'should; ought; may'

has a clear-cut optative function. It introduces clauses whose verb is in the infinitive, and which express a wish:

(39) *Zol er shoyn kumen.* ("Let him come already.")

In this example, taken out of context, there is no basis for deciding whether the coming is anxiously welcomed by the speaker, or else merely looked forward to with resignation. To convey such nuances, something further must be added:

(40) *Zol er shoyn kumen gezunterhéyt.* (lit. "Let him come already, in good health.").

Here we understand that the person's coming is eagerly anticipated. But:

(41) *Zol er shoyn kumen, in drerd aráyn.* (lit. "Let him come already, into the earth / into hell [with him]," i.e. "Let him come, damn him, we'll cope somehow.").

In this latter case it is obvious that one's basic attitude toward the person and his coming is a hostile one.

Sometimes the speaker's attitude is already abundantly clear from the verb of the complement clause itself:

(42) *Zol er matsliekh zayn in dem eysek.* ("May he succeed in that affair.")

(43) *Zol er dervorgn vern.* ("May he be strangled.")

(44) *Zol ikh nor derlebn tsu zen azá zakh.* ("May I only live to see such a thing.").

Often the auxiliary verb *lozn* 'let' is used instead of optative *zoln:*

(45) *Loz zi vartn a bisl mer -- vos art dos aykh?* ("Let her wait a little longer -- what do you care?").

(b) *halevái + Clause. Halevái* is a word whose only function is to indicate that the following clause is a *wish* (often a wish that the speaker feels is unlikely to be fulfilled).[40] The optative clause itself may have any of a number of internal structures. It may contain *zoln* + infinitival complement:

(46) *Haleváy zol gut zayn.* ("May it turn out all right.")

It may contain a verb in the present tense understood to refer to the future:

(47) *Haleváy brengt er epes a matone far di kinder.*
("I hope he brings some kind of present for the children.")

It may contain an overt future-tense VP, consisting of the auxiliary verb *veln* + infinitive:

(48) *Haleváy vet er zikh oykh kenen aríbergànvenen dem grenets.*
("I hope he'll be able to sneak across the border too.")

(49) *Haleváy vet er zikh tsebrekhn hent un fis.* ("I hope he breaks every bone in his body" [lit. "hands and feet"].)

It may contain only an adjective, with deleted copula:

(50) *Haleváy vayter nit erger.* ("I hope it gets no worse" [lit. "optative + further-not-worse"].)

To express a wish whose fulfillment is doubtful, or which is manifestly hopeless, the clause may contain the conditional marker *volt* + past participle:

(51) *Haleváy volt es yo gevén, vi mir hobn gehóft.* ("I wish it *had* turned out the way we had hoped." [*See also sentence 113, below.*])

Haleváy may occur as an utterance all by itself, in response to a statement or wish expressed by someone else. Thus at a funeral one is likely to take leave of one's fellow-mourners like this:

(52a) *Mir zoln zikh zen oyf simkhes.* ("We should meet [hereafter] on happier occasions.") / (52b) *Haleváy.* ("I hope so.")

In this 'interjectory' usage, *haleváy* is often reinforced by a following *oméyn* 'amen':

(53) *Haleváy oméyn!* ("I fervently hope so!")[41]

(c) *oyf* + NP + *gezógt (gevorn).* One of the commonest petitive structures specifies the person affected by the wish (let us call him the

wishificiary) by making him the object of the preposition *oyf* *(af* in
normal rapid speech) 'on, upon,' with this phrase then followed by the
periphrastic passive participle *gezógt gevorn* '[may it] have been
said.' The combined meaning is 'may the object or event in question
belong to or affect this wishificiary, in such a way that people will
speak of them in the same breath.'[42]

Depending on the speaker's underlying attitude toward the wishificiary, these expressions may be either bono- or malo-petitive. If
the object of *oyf* is *mir* 'me,' the sentence is auto-bono-petitive, and
generally conveys a rather covetous attitude toward something good
that is in another's possession:

(54) *Oyf mir gezógt gevorn azá sheyne heym!* ("I wish *I* had such a
beautiful home!" [lit. "Of me it should be said that I have such a
beautiful home."]).

If the wishificiary is first person plural (*undz* 'us,' *úndzere kinder*
'our children,' etc.), the expression is intermediate between auto-
and allo-bono-petition, since both oneself and others are involved.
If the wishificiary is a second or third person to whom one is well-
disposed, the expression is allo-bono-petitive:

(55) *A khvat Betsalel,* [*mir*] *óysgeboyt a krêtshmele, oyf ale mayne
gute fraynt gezógt.* ("Hurray for Betsalel, he built [me] a little
inn, like all my good friends should have!"; "May it be said of all
my good friends that they have a little inn like the one Betsalel
built for me, God bless him." RP, p. 175.).

If, on the other hand, one is hostile to the wishificiary, the expression is allo-malo-petitive [*see below, section 9*]:

(56) *Oyf mayne sonim gezógt gevorn, vi 's baysn mir di fis fun der
krópeve.* ("My feet are so itchy from this poison ivy, like it should
be said of my enemies.")

(d) *azá yor oyf + NP.* This expression is similar to the preceding,
but more restricted in use. In Jewish culture considerable importance
is attached to the concept of 'a year's run of luck' or 'the good or
bad things that can happen to you in the course of a year.' One hopes

to have *a gut yor,* 'a good year.' This phrase is used formulaically
as a return greeting to such salutations as *gutn ovnt* 'Good evening':

(57a) *Gutn ovnt.* ("Good evening.")

(57b) *Gutn ovnt. A gut yor.* ("Good evening and a good year.")

The opposite of a *gut yor* is a *shvarts yor* 'black year,' or a *fintster
yor* 'dark year.'[43] It is a grievous insult to wish someone a bad year.
This preoccupation with the *year* as the temporal unit in which fortune
and misfortune are parcelled out seems certainly to be based in Jewish
religious tradition. *Rósheshone* 'New Year's Day' is one of the most
important holidays of the year. Ten days later, on *Yom Kiper,* God is
thought to decide irrevocably what the fate of a man shall be throughout the coming year. Each year, God takes another look at a person's
deeds, and draws up a new contract for the next year's luck on the
basis of his performance during the past year.[44]

It is in this light that *azá yor oyf + NP* 'such a year on NP'
is to be understood. Typically this expression precedes a clause introduced by the conjunction *vi* 'as; how; the way that,' wherein the
state of affairs that is wished for is described. When the wishificiary NP is first person, the meaning is auto-bono-petitive:

(58) *Azá yor oyf mir, vi er fort arúm di gantse velt.* ("It should
only happen to me, the way he travels around the whole world."
[lit. "May such a year (during which I would do wondrous things) fall
to my lot, the way *he* travels around the whole world."])

(59) *Azá yor oyf mir, vi er klaybt nakhes fun di éyneklekh.* ("It
should only happen to me, the way he gets joy from his grandchildren.")

With a first-person wishificiary, the implication is that the
wished-for state of affairs is unlikely ever to come to pass. The
petitive phrase is the expression of a feeling of rather impotent
envy: 'if only I had luck like his.'[45]

With a non-first person wishificiary, the nuances are quite different. Here the speaker is usually being allo-malo-petitive. The

situation or action described in the *vi*-clause is something the speaker resents, and he is vengefully hoping that the wishificiary will have to suffer misfortune ('such a [bad, dark, black] year') because of it:

(60) *Azá yor oyf im, vi er hot mir óngepatshket dem ksavyád.* ("He should have such a year [as would pay him back for] the way he made a mess of my manuscript!")

6.0 BONO-PETITION

We now proceed to locutions that are specifically bono-petitive, rather than merely petitive in general. These are almost always *allo-*petitive; if you are wishing for good things for yourself (auto-bono-petition), you must usually use one of the more general devices discussed in the previous section.[46] There is no harm in referring to allo-bono-petition by the simpler term *blessing,* and to the person being blessed as the *beneficiary.*

Blessing people is a fine art in Yiddish. It is possible to weave infinite variations on the various benedictive themes. Although the most baroque flights of bono-petitive eloquence are reserved for special occasions like marriages and graduations, the more common and formulaic expressions are thickly sprinkled into everyday conversation as a kind of interpersonal psychic lubricant. They are a vital part of the language.

The usual Yiddish words for 'to bless' are *vintshn zikh* (lit. 'wish for one another; wish for oneself'),[47] and *bentshn* (ult. < Latin *benedicere*).[48] A more vigorous verb is *ónbentshn* 'to bless thoroughly,' with an intensive aspectual prefix:

(61) *Oy, hot zi mikh óngebentsht!* ("Boy, did she ever bless me up and down!")

All Yiddish blessings revolve around certain key desiderata, the good things of life. These include, first and foremost, *lebn* 'life' and *lange yor* 'longevity.' But what is life if one is too debilitated to enjoy it?[49] Equally important are *gezúnt* 'health' and *koyekh* 'strength' (or *shtark zayn* 'being strong'). Still there is no particular joy in living, even if one is healthy and strong, if you don't know where your next meal is coming from. As the proverb has it:

(62) *Orem iz keyn shand -- ober oykh keyn groyser koved nit.* ("Poverty is no disgrace -- but no great honor either." YP, p. 98.)

One therefore wishes for *parnose* 'livelihood, a good living, prosperity.' And yet money isn't everything either. What good is money if you have no children to spend it on and share it with? As they say:

(63) *Kinder un gelt iz a sheyne velt.* ("Children and money make a beautiful world.")

One of the richest of all life's treasures is *nakhes,* a peculiarly Jewish concept that is as hard to render in English as Chinese *hsiao* (which usually gets translated as 'filial piety'). *Nakhes,* used most commonly to mean *nakhes fun di kinder* ('child-*nakhes*') is the satisfaction that parents derive from the accomplishments of their children.[50] As far as *nakhes*-providing potential goes, anything may be an 'accomplishment' (growing one's permanent teeth, becoming *bar-mitsve,* marrying a Jewish spouse, playing the violin for company, etc.). Children provide their parents with the most *nakhes* when they are small.[51] When they grow up, they are likely to pose more problems:

(64) *Kleyne kinder, kleyne freydn -- groyse kinder, groyse tsores.* ("Little children, little joys -- big children, big troubles.")[52]

When this happens, the best one can hope for is *nakhes fun di éyneklekh* or '*nakhes* from grandchildren.'[53]

When one is fortunate enough to have all these good things, it can be said that one has *glik* or *mazl* 'good luck.' To wish someone luck in this sense is a shorthand way of evoking all the desiderata we have mentioned. Similarly, to wish someone *a gut yor* 'a good year' is to express the hope that his luck will hold (or improve) throughout the foreseeable future [*above 5.0d*].

6.1   *Classification By Desiderata*

Some of the most frequently encountered blessings are given in the following list.[54] Note that the optative auxiliary verb *zoln* [*above 5.0a*] appears in most of them. Where it does not occur on the surface (especially in verbless blessings) we may claim that it is down there in the deep structure, if it gives us *nakhes* to do so:[55]

(a) *Life and longevity*

(65) *A lebn tsu dir! / A lebn oyf dir!*[56] ("Life to you!"; "Long life to you!")

(66) *Lang lebn zolstu!* ("Long may you live!")[57]

(67) *Yorn dir!* ("Years [of life] to you!")

This, as well as the following (68), is used particularly when blessing children:

(68) *A zeyde / bobe zolstu zayn!* ("May you [live to] be a grand-father / grandmother!")

(69) *Zolstu derlebn tsu + Clause!* ("May you live to Clause!")

The clause may describe any desirable eventuality. The following is one random example:

(69a) *Zolstu derlebn tsu firn dayne kinder un kinds kinder tsu der khupe.* ("May you live to lead your children and children's children to the wedding-canopy.")

(b) *Health*

(70) *Zay gezúnt!* ("Be healthy!")

This is perhaps the commonest formula for leave-taking, and is also usable as the closing to a telephone conversation.[58]

(71) *Zolstu zayn gezúnt! / Gezúnt zolstu zayn!* ("May you be healthy!"). Both variants are equally common.

(72) *A gezúnt tsu dir!* (lit. "A health to you!")

(73) *Tsu gezúnt!*

This is frequently used to a sneezer[59], like 'English' *gesundheit!*
Often, however, it means *May it do your health good!*, and is used to
someone who is ingesting food or medicine. In this latter sense, it
is an abbreviation of (74):

(74) *Zol dir zayn tsu gezúnt!* ("May it do your health good.")

(75) *A gezúnt dir in kop / képele!*[60] ("A health to your head /
little head!"). Said especially to children.

(76) *A gezúnt dir in yeder éyverl!* ("A health to all your little
body-parts!"). Tender, used especially to children.[61]

(77) *A gréptsele aróys, a gezúntele aráyn!* ("A burpie-wurpie out,
and a healthie-wealthie in!"). Said after successfully burping a
baby.[62]

(c) *Nakhes; a year's luck; combination-blessings*

(78) *Zolstu hobn nakhes fun dayne kinder!* ("May you have *nakhes*
from your children.")

Instead of *hobn* 'have,' one may use the verbs *klaybn* 'gather' or *shepn*
'scoop up' with *nakhes*. These metaphorically concrete verbs point up
the quality of palpable reality that the concept of *nakhes* has traditionally had in Jewish culture.

(79) *A gut yor zolstu hobn!* ("May you have a good year!")

    Often one touches several benedictive bases at once, mentioning
more than one of the desiderata:

(80) *Got zol dir nor gebn gezúnt un koyekh!* ("May God only give
you health and strength!")[63]

(81) *Zolstu zayn gezúnt un shtark un raykh un freylekh!* ("May you
be healthy and strong and rich and happy!")

(82) *Zol dir Got gebn glik mit parnose mit lange yor.* ("May God give you luck and a good living and long years of life!")

(83) *Got zol gebn, ir zolt zayn gezúnt un ir zolt vern vos a tog raykher!* ("May God grant that you be healthy, and become richer every day!" RP, p. 118.)

(84) *Mir zoln ale derlebn iber a yor gezunterhéyt, nor zol zayn sholem oyf der velt!* ("May we all live through another year in good health, and may there only be peace in the world!")

These multiple or all-purpose blessings are for rather serious occasions, like leave-takings, embarking on new enterprises, etc. It is as if the blesser were afraid of leaving anything out. He wants to be sure that God, who can be very mysterious in His ways, won't be left any loopholes through which He could sneak in some misfortune or other. Thus if one prays for wealth alone, one can lose one's health. What good is that?

An interesting specialized use of a combination-blessing occurs when one interrupts what someone else is saying. To soften the rudeness you can pronounce a formula that includes the blessing *mir zoln lebn in nakhes un freyd* ("May we live in pleasure and joy."). This particular blessing is chosen because it rhymes with *reyd* 'speech':

(85) *Ikh shlog dir iber di reyd -- mir zoln lebn in nakhes un freyd.* ("I have interrupted your speech -- pleasures and joys our lives should reach!" *L'Chayim,* p. 94.)[64]

6.2 *Action-Oriented Blessings and God's Help*

The blessings we have discussed so far have been of the general existential type: wishes that the beneficiary might prosper in his life in general. A further semantic type of bono-petitive expression may be distinguished, where the aid of God is invoked to help the beneficiary perform some specific action (or cope with a specific situation) in a successful way.   These expressions all involve a word for God (*Got* 'God,' *der Éybershter* 'the One on high,' *der Boyre-borkhu* 'the Creator, blessed be He,' *Reboyne-sheloylem* 'the Lord of the universe,' etc.), and the verb *helfn* 'help' or *gebn* 'give.' The expression may be either *optative*, with the auxiliary verb *zoln* plus infinitive; or *conditional*, with the conjunction *az* 'if' and the conditional auxiliary *volt* plus infinitive or past participle.[65]

(86) *Got zol gebn az vos ir vet ónheybn tsu ton, zolt ir ton on a sof.* ("May God grant that whatever you start to do you may do endlessly." RP, p. 111.)

(87) *Es iz a sakónedike krenk, nor az der Éybershter volt gebn, er zol a bisl shvitsn, volt er nokh geként gezúnt vern.* ("It is a dangerous illness, but if God grants that he should sweat a little bit, he could still get well." RP, p. 109.)

These expressions may be auto-petitive as well. One can be requesting God's aid on one's own behalf:

(88) *Az Got volt helfn, un ikh zol gefinen afn gas a tóyznter, volt ikh gevén zeyer tsufridn.* ("If God should help me, and I find a thousand [ruble] note on the street, I would be very satisfied." RP, p. 80.)

Sometimes when God's help is invoked, the intent is just as much allo-malo-recognitive as it is allo-bono-petitive. That is, the speaker means the phrase to be interpreted as simultaneously sympathetic and well-wishing. Consider the following example (with the synonymous but more archaic *lozn* 'let' instead of *zoln*), where a creditor hypocritically uses such an expression to his debtor with this dual intent:

(89) *Reb Yisroel, meyle ir hot óngezetst, loz aykh Got helfn, ober mayn gmiles-khesed darft ir dokh avékgebn.* ("Well, Reb Yisroel,[66] you've gone bankrupt, God help you, but you've still got to pay me back my loan."[67] RP, p. 108.)

Very often an action-oriented blessing takes the form of the imperative of a verb plus the adverb *gezunterhéyt* 'in good health':[68]

(90) *Es gezunterhéyt, mayn kind.* ("Eat in good health, my child.")[69]

(91) *For gezunterhéyt, un hit zikh op far shikurim.* ("Drive in good health, and watch out for drunks.")

Many such expressions have the status of set formulas. Thus when someone puts on a new garment for the first time, people should say to him:

(92) *Trog (es) gezunterhéyt.*[70] ("Wear it in good health.")

When someone is leaving your house and is expected back later (whether in five minutes or five years), you should say:

(93) *Gey gezunterhéyt un kum gezunterhéyt.* ("Go in good health and come [back] in good health.")[71]

If someone has just said *Gey gezunterhéyt* to you, the proper reply to make to him, if he is staying behind, is:

(93a) *Blayb gezunterhéyt.* ("Stay in good health.")

Instead of an imperative, one often finds *zoln* plus infinitive with *gezunterhéyt* [see sentence (40) above].[72]

6.3 *Parenthetical Blessings*

Many of the general existential blessings we have just seen [*6.1 a, b*], and some others besides, may be manipulated in a characteristically Yiddish way. They may be inserted parenthetically into larger sentences, where they modify the beneficiary noun-phrase rather in the manner of a Homeric epithet. Instead of 'rosy-fingered dawn' and 'far-shooting Apollo' we have locutions like 'my son, may he live and be well' or 'my granddaughter, a life to her little head.' These parenthetical blessings are typically uttered unthinkingly, by a sort of reflex action:

(94) *Shver, lebn zolt ir, haynt hobn mir yontev.* ("Father-in-law, may you live, today is a holiday." RP, p. 102.)

The father-in-law has done nothing specific to merit this blessing --

he is the man's father-in-law, that's all.[73]

(95)   *Dos hot úfgeton mayn kadesh, biz hundert un tsvantsik yor.*
("That's the work of my son, may he live to be 120 years old.")[74]

(96)   *Ot geyt mayn eyn un éyntsiker éynikl, a lebn tsu zayn kop.*
("There goes my one and only grandchild, a life to his head.")

Most common of all these formulas is probably *zol(n) gezúnt zayn*
"may [he, she, they] be healthy." Note the lack of a pronoun ana-
phoric to the beneficiary:[75]

(97)   *Hot fun der geshikhte gehért der rov, zol gezúnt zayn.* ("So
the rabbi, may he be healthy, heard about the whole business." RP,
pp. 75-6.)

(98)   *Fun ershtn man hob ikh fir kínderlekh, zoln gezúnt zayn.*
("With my first husband I had four children, may they be healthy."
RP, p. 141.)

(99)   *Mit mayn tatn, zol gezúnt zayn, hot zikh amól getrofn punkt
azá mayse.* ("The exact same thing once happened to my father, may
he be healthy." RP, p. 140.)

(100)   *Ayer vayb, zol gezúnt zayn, vet oykh kenen kokhn a tepl on a
diplóm.* ("Your wife, may she be healthy, will be able to cook a pot
[of food] just as well without a diploma.")[76]

Automatic though these parenthetical expressions are, they may
easily be activated into the speaker's consciousness, and even exploit-
ed for humorous purposes. Witness the following joke,[77] where a marriage broker is trying to convince a reluctant young man about the
joys of the wedded state:

(101)   *...On a vayb iz úmetik, iz men elnd vi a shteyn. Ober az me
hot a vayb, vi ba mir in shtub lemoshl (zol zi gezúnt un shtark
zayn!) iz gor an ander lebn ... Zi makht a gutn ónbaysn ... (zol zi
gezúnt un shtark zayn biz hundert un tsvantsik yor!) ... un zi zitst
un kukt aykh on mit ire kóshere éygelekh un shmeykhlt aykh tsu ...
(zol zi lebn!). Dernókh zitst ir zikh tsuzamen un shmuest ... un zi*

redt zikh, un ir hert zikh ayn, un zi redt -- un zi redt -- un zi
redt un zi redt un zi redt! <u>*A fayer zol ir trefn vi zi redt!*</u>
("Without a wife it's lonesome, you're as miserable as a stone. But
when you've got a wife, like I have in my house, for example (*may*
she be healthy and strong!), it's a completely different life ...
She makes you a good breakfast ... (*may she be healthy and strong un-*
til she's 120!) ... and she sits and looks at you with her sweet
little eyes and smiles at you ... (*may she live!*). Then you sit together and chat ... and she talks, and you listen, and she talks --
and she talks -- and she talks and she talks and she talks! *May a*
fire take her the way she talks!")

The exquisite humor here resides in the totally unexpected shift from
bono-petitive formulas to the rousing malo-petitive one at the end.
The marriage-broker has painted such a vivid picture of his own married
life that his true feelings burst through to the surface despite himself.

Parenthetical blessings may also function in another way. They
may be used to soften a reproach, or to take the sting out of one's
contradiction of another's words, or to apologize for something unpleasant that must be said. The idea is something like 'despite the
unwelcomeness of the message I must give you, I am still fundamentally
well-disposed towards you.' We may call these *palliative blessings:*

(102) *"Efsher hot ir a shtikl fish?" "Zolt ir gezúnt zayn, keyn*
fish iz haynt nitó, morgn vet mistome zayn." (" 'Maybe you have a
little piece of fish?' 'May you be healthy, there's no fish today,
perhaps tomorrow there will be.' " RP, p. 141.)

(103) *Oy, zolstu gezúnt zayn, vos far a patshkeráy hostu do gemákht!*
("Oh, you should be healthy, what a mess you've made here!")

(104) *Gezúnt un shtark zol er zayn, der alter -- er veys shoyn gor*
nit, vos er redt. ("He should be healthy and strong, the old man --
he doesn't know what he's saying any more." RP, p. 103.)

(105) *Zolstu gezúnt zayn, Yankl, vos darfstu zikh mishn tsvishn*

fremde layt? ("May you be healthy, Yankl, why do you have to go around mixing in strangers' business?")

(106) *Ze, zolstu gezúnt zayn -- az du host shoyn ye azá rakhmones, to loz dem mentshn aráyn!* ("Look here, may you be healthy -- if you do already feel such pity, then let the man inside!" RP, p. 114.)

(107) *"Ikh farshtéy nit. Ir zayt aléyn a shnayder, far vos farríkht ir nit ayer kapote?" Makht der shnayder, "Zolt ir gezúnt zayn -- fun vanen zol ikh hobn tsayt tsu farríkhtn mayn éygene kapote?"* (" 'I don't understand. You're a tailor yourself, so why don't you fix your own coat?' So the tailor said, 'May you be healthy -- where am I going to get the time to fix my own coat?' " RP, p. 89.)

The last example is an instance of the 'patient explanation of the obvious' type of palliative blessing. The tailor is assuming the pose of superior knowledge -- <u>he</u> knows perfectly well why he doesn't fix his own coat. His interlocutor has asked a stupid question. It is almost as if the tailor were embarrassed at the other man's ignorance. He therefore tempers any tendency he might have to give an acerbic reply by using the benedictive formula.[78]

6.4 *Theo-Bono-Petitives: Liturgical Blessings*

It is possible not only to bless oneself, or other people, but also to bless God and His holy name. In traditional Jewish life, ritual blessings (in Hebrew) were prescribed by religious law to accompany dozens of everyday actions, in order that one's daily life be suffused by a sense of divine providence.[79] Such a blessing is called a *brokhe*. Although their underlying motivation is certainly bono-recognitive (acknowledging that existence itself as well as all human activities are divine gifts), *brokhes* are quasi-petitive in form. All ritual blessings begin with the words *borúkh ató adoynóy*[80] 'blessed art Thou, O Lord.' God does not need our praise -- or does He? At any rate, the following *brokhe*, to be uttered when putting on a new garment for the first time, will serve as an example:

(108) *Borúkh ató adoynóy, eloyhenu melekh ho-oylóm, malbísh arumím.*
("Blessed art Thou, O Lord our God, King of the Universe, who clothest the naked.")

According to ancient custom, if a Jew hears another person reciting a
brokhe, he chimes in with ritual responses at two points: after the
first three words, and at the end.

(108a) *Borúkh ató adoynóy* -- ("Blessed art Thou, O Lord -- ")

(108b) -- *borúkh hu u-vorúkh shemóy* -- ("blessed be He and blessed
be His name -- ")

(108a) -- *eloyhenu melekh ho-oylóm, malbísh arumím.* (" -- our God,
King of the Universe, who clothest the naked.")

(108b) *Oméyn.* ("Amen.")

It is perhaps neither far-fetched nor sacrilegious to view *borúkh hu
u-vorúkh shemóy* as a parenthetical blessing in the sense of 6.3 above.
It is as if one were saying 'God, He should live and be well, has done
this for us!' It would be interesting to undertake a serious investigation into the historical and psychological relationships between
secular parenthetical blessings and these liturgical parenthetical
ones.[81]

The response at the end, *oméyn*, has of course found its way into
all European languages. In Yiddish it is not confined to liturgical
use, but is an appropriate response to any non-parenthetical petitive
expression:[82]

(109a) *Zol er lang lebn, un zayn gezúnt.* ("May he live long and
be healthy.")

(109b) *Oméyn!* ("Amen to that!")

Many other responses to a blessing are possible. When someone wishes
you well, you may graciously reply:

(110) *Fun dayn moyl in Gots óyern!* ("From your mouth into God's
ears!", i.e. "may God harken to your wishes!")[83]

If you wish to return good for good, and offer a counter-blessing in return, you may say:

(111)   *Zol dir zayn gut vi du vintshst zikh aléyn!*   ("May things go as well for you as you yourself wish [for me]!")[84]

If someone has congratulated you for some notable happy event, like the marriage of a child, you may return the good wishes by saying:

(112)   *In gikhn bay aykh óptsugebn!*   ("[May I] soon [have occasion to] return [such a blessing] to you!", i.e. "May *your* child soon get married too!")[85]

6.5   *Ironical Commentaries on the Petitive Attitude*

Despite all the bono-petitive expressions with which Yiddish speakers pepper their conversation, they are under no illusions that 'wishing makes it so.' Life is in fact hard, and all our prayers and entreaties and bono-petitions are ultimately powerless to affect our fate. Ironic proverbs to this effect abound:

(113)   *Halevány volt es azóy yo gevén, vi es vet nit zayn.*   ("Would that it were the way it will not be." YP, p. 82.)[86]

(114)   *Ven es zol helfn Got betn, volt men shoyn tsúgedungen mentshn.* ("If praying to God did any good, they would've already hired people to do it." YP, p. 112.)

(115)   *Got vet helfn -- vi helft nor Got biz Got vet helfn.*   ("God will help -- but how will God help until He gets around to helping?"; i.e. "God help us until He gets around to helping!" YP, p. 112.)

(116)   *Got hot lib dem oremán un helft dem nogid.*   ("God loves the poor and helps the rich." YP, p. 80.)

In a less cosmic and more humorous vein, there is a whole set of proverb variants to the effect that wishing can't change anything. They all involve one's grandmother. In the most innocent version, the one found in books of proverbs, it goes like this:

(117) *Oyb di bobe volt gehát a bord, volt zi gevén a zeyde.* ("If
grandmother had had a beard, she would've been a grandfather.")[87]

More fanciful is the following variant:

(118) *Oyb di bobe volt gehát reder, volt zi gevén a vogn.* ("If
grandmother had had wheels, she would've been a wagon.")[88]

The version I myself learned first may or may not have been the original one:

(119) *Oyb di bobe volt gehát eyer, volt zi gevén a zeyde.* ("If
grandmother had had balls, she would've been a grandfather.")[89]

7.0   MALO-FUGITION: DELIVER US FROM EVIL!

The mirror image of good-seeking (bono-petition) is evil-shunning
(malo-fugition). At some psychological level they are the same thing.
One is the *via positiva* and the other is the *via negativa* to the elusive goal of human happiness.[90] In this section, we are concerned
with overt expressions of the malo-fugitive attitude in Yiddish.

Probably all peoples indulge in *apotropaism* to some extent in
their lives and linguistic behavior.[91] Yet this was a particularly
striking feature of traditional Yiddish-speaking society in Eastern
Europe. It is not hard to see why an oppressed, ghettoized people
should have been so preoccupied with the precariousness of life and
the ubiquitousness of evil. Malo-fugitive expressions abound in Yiddish. It would take a cultural historian to do a proper job of dis-
entangling the diverse influences which they reflect: the beliefs and
customs of the Gentile peasantry among whom the Jews lived; attitudes
deriving from Jewish religious tradition, some of which are undoubtedly
traceable back to the ancient Near East; and existential attitudes
which the Jews share with people everywhere, by virtue of their common
humanity.

We shall organize our discussion around the various *techniques
for avoidance of evil* that Yiddish malo-fugitives imply by their

linguistic form: ignoring evil in the hope that it will go away; pronouncing otherwise meaningless magic words; invoking God's protection;
keeping a low profile so as not to tempt the fates, or not complaining
lest an even worse disaster befall; exorcising the demons of ill-
fortune; finding scapegoats to absorb the evil in one's stead; and
appeasing the dead.

Almost all malo-fugitive expressions in Yiddish may be used parenthetically, and are equally suitable for turning aside evil from
oneself (*auto-malo-fugition*) or from others (*allo-malo-fugition*).

7.1 *Banishing the Evil from Consciousness*

Human beings, like ostriches, have a strong tendency to combat
evil by pointedly ignoring it. It is this psychological mechanism
which is behind the linguistic device of *euphemism*.[92]
A common Yiddish greeting is:

(120) *Vos hert zikh guts?* ("What do you hear that's good?")

That is, don't tell me anything that will bring me down! Accentuate
the positive, eliminate the negative. A cemetery is frequently
referred to as *dos gute ort* 'the good place' -- maybe if we call it
good, we won't have to live there for a while yet. In the Litvish
(Northeastern) dialect, a common way of asking somebody where he lives
is:

(121) *Vu freyt ir zikh?* ("Where are you happy?")

This strange expression is a euphemism for *vu voynt ir (vu veynt ir*
in Litvish dialect) 'where do you live?', because of the accidental
homophony between *veynen (=voynen)* 'to dwell', and *veynen* 'to weep'
(German *wohnen* and *weinen*, respectively).

Euphemisms aside, Yiddish has other malo-fugitive expressions
which specifically say that a certain event is so unpleasant that it
is not to be thought of, or not to be spoken of, or not to be known
of:[93]

(a) *nit/nisht far* NP *gedákht*.[94] This phrase means 'not to be
thought of in connection with NP.' The NP is often a personal pronoun. When it is first person it is auto-fugitive; otherwise it is
allo-fugitive, as in the following examples:

(122) *Eynem fun di yidn iz gegangen, nit far* <u>*aykh*</u> *gedákht, zeyer
shlekht.* ("For one of these Jews things went -- may it be unthinkable in your case -- very badly." RP, p. 80.)

(123) *Es hot zikh amól getrofn, az a shif iz gegangen afn yam un iz
gevorn, nit far* <u>*aykh*</u> *gedákht, a shtarker vind.* ("It once happened
that a ship went to sea, and there arose -- may it be unthinkable in
your case -- a strong wind." RP, p. 71.)

(124) *In a tsayt arúm iz gevorn in shtot a mageyfe oyf tsign.
Zaynen óysgeshtorbn, nit far* <u>*aykh*</u> *gedákht, ale tsign in shtot.*
("After a while a plague on goats broke out in town. So every goat
in town -- may it be unthinkable in your case -- died." RP,
pp. 36-7.)

The intent of the formula is to insure that in recounting the misfortune that befell someone else, the speaker is not endangering his
listener by any evil spin-off or fall-out. Somewhat different is the
next example:

(125) *Der balabós fun der akhsanye iz gevén, nit far* <u>*aykh*</u> *gedákht,
a groyser amorets.* ("The innkeeper was -- and I don't mean any in-
vidious comparisons with you -- a complete ignoramus." RP, p. 148.)

Here there is no question of the listener being adversely affected
by the innkeeper's ignorance. One is, after all, either an ignoramus
or one isn't. Rather the idea is 'it is unthinkable to mention you
and this ignoramus in the same breath.'[95]

Other common fillers of the NP slot in this formula are *keynem*
'nobody,' *keyn yidn* 'no Jew,' *keyn mentshn* 'no person,' and, most
altruistically and emphatically, *mayne sonim* 'my enemies'[96]:

(126) *Itst zitst er un reykhert marikhvane a gantsn tog, nisht far
<u>keynem</u> gedákht.* ("And now he sits and smokes marijuana all day

long -- may it be unthinkable for anyone.")

(127) *Un vifl es iz gevén mentshn in shif zaynen, nit far keyn yidn
gedákht, dertrunken gevorn.* ("And all the people who were on the
ship -- may it be unthinkable for all Jews -- were drowned."
RP, p. 71.)

(128) *In a shtetl hot me gerédt oyf eyner a yídene, az zi hot
asokim, nit far keyn yidn gedákht, mit a póylishn poyer.* ("In a
town it was said of a certain Jewish woman that she was having re-
lations -- may it be unthinkable for all Jews -- with a Polish
peasant.")

(129) *Un gevén iz er a kaptsn, nit far keyn mentshn gedákht.* ("And
he was a pauper -- may it be unthinkable for any person.")

(130) *Er hot nebekh farlorn vayb un kinder, nisht far mayne sonim
gedákht.* ("He lost, poor man, his wife and children -- may it be
unthinkable [even] for my enemies.")

The formulaic nature of these expressions is demonstrated by
their appearance in sentences where they are logically absurd -- where
there is absolutely no hope that the evil can be avoided by banishing
it from consciousness, simply because it is inevitable:

(131) *Mayn vayb hot ir dokh geként. Iz zi, nit far keyn yidn
gedákht, geshtorbn.* ("You knew my wife, of course. Well, she
died -- may it be unthinkable for all Jews." RP, p. 22.)

(b) *nit oyf NP gezógt gevorn.* We have seen above [5.0c] that the un-
negated expression *oyf NP gezógt gevorn* 'may it be said of NP' is a
common bono-petitive formula. With the negative added, it becomes
a malo-fugitive one, of the *banishing from consciousness* type:

(132) *Iz zikh meyashev zayn vayb un vert, nit oyf aykh gezógt
gevorn, krank.* ("So his wife took it into her head and -- may it
not be said of you -- got sick." RP, p. 138.)[97]

It seems likely that this expression ultimately reflects a belief in
the blind workings of *fate:*

(133) *Nor vu iz dos gezógt gevorn, az ikh vel shtarbn [in der milkhome]?* ("But where is it said that I will die [in the war]?" RP, p. 61.)

This formula seems to contain an oblique reference to the legendary divine book where God keeps a record of men's fates for the coming year [*see above 5.0d*].

(c) *me zol nit visn (fun).* Just as some things are too awful to be thought about (*gedákht*) or spoken of (*gezógt*), they are also too un- pleasant to *know* about. The expression *me zol nit visn* 'one should not know' is construed with the preposition *fun* 'about, of, from'[98] and may appear in the main clause of its sentence:

(134) *Me zol nit visn fun azoyne tsores.* ("We shouldn't know about such troubles.")

When the *fun + Object* is pronominalized into *derfún* 'of it, about it, thereof,' the expression may be introduced parenthetically into another clause:

(135) *Un dortn in Índie hot er zikh óngenumen mit der tsoraas, me zol nit visn derfún.* ("And there in India he caught leprosy, we shouldn't know from it.")

7.2 *Pronouncing the Magic Word kholile and its Relatives*

One of the most frequently encountered psycho-ostensives of them all is *kholile*, an otherwise meaningless word whose only semantic component is [+ malo-fugition]. It is originally a Hebrew word, and appears in the Bible.[99] In Yiddish it is extensively used to indicate the speaker's abhorrence for a certain event or state of affairs. The event in question may be of the utmost gravity, or may be relatively trivial; and the speaker's abhorrence may be quite genuine or ob- viously ironic. Typically *kholile* is inserted into its sentence just before the stigmatized event is mentioned, though it may also occur as an utterance by itself in response to something that has just been

said. First some examples of *kholile* in its straightforward malo-
fugitive guise:

(136) *Di mume hot óngehoybn moyre tsu hobn, tsi iz der bokher*
kholile nit baym zinen. ("The aunt began to be afraid that the
young man might be -- horrors! -- out of his mind." RP,
p. 35.)[100,101]

(137) *Er iz kholile nit orem gevorn, ober gelt iz dokh káylekhdik.*
("He didn't -- horrors! -- become poor, but you know money is
round." RP, p. 93.)[102]

(138) *Veyst dokh, az ikh bin kholile keyn shiker nit -- ikh bin nit*
azóy loet nokh a bisl bronfn. ("But you must know that I'm not --
horrors! -- a drunkard. I'm not so greedy for a little brandy."
RP, p. 107.)

(139) *Di kinder ... zoln nit tsu fil shtifn, kholile, un bifrát*
[zolt ir zey] óyslernen a bisl derekh-erets. ("The children
shouldn't fool around too much -- horrors! -- and especially [you
should] teach [them] a little proper respect." RP, p. 6.)[103]

(140) *Der yid hot zikh shtilerhéyt óysgeton un shtilerhéyt avékge-*
legt, der generál zol kholile nit hern un nit úfgevekt vern. ("The
Jew undressed quietly and quietly lay down, so that the general
wouldn't -- horrors! -- hear him and wake up." RP, p. 144.)

(141) *Háyntike tsaytn yogn zikh di yunge layt nokh nokh meydlekh,*
tsi kholile gor nokh shikses, un der kop ligt zey nit in lernen.
("Nowadays the young people go chasing after girls, or even --
horrors! -- after Gentile girls, and their heads are not concerned
with [sacred] learning." RP, p. 41.)

(142) *A vits ken kholile khorev makhn a velt.* ("A joke can --
horrors! -- lay waste a world." RP, p. 173.)

In the following example, the bono-recognitive formula *borkhashém*
[*above 3.0*] is juxtaposed to *kholile* with humorous effect -- the good
is recognized and the bad is abhorred in one fell swoop:

(143) *Der yid hot geknéytsht dem shtern un hot gekvétsht dem moyekh -- vorem ir must visn, az er hot, borkhashém, gehát vos tsu kvetshn, kholile nit keyn puster kop.* ("The Jew wrinkled his brow and racked his brain -- from which you can see that he had, thank God, something to rack, not -- horrors! -- an empty head." RP, p. 93.)

Fairly often we find *kholile* used in a sarcastic way, so that the abhorrence is not genuine, but merely feigned for effect. The person who ostensibly feels the abhorrence is understood to be a hypocrite:

(144) *Mer nit, er flegt a mol a bísele tsu gánvenen. Dos heyst, fun késhene flegt er kholile nit gánvenen, nor in geshéft flegt er gebn a kapetshke falshe vog.* ("The only thing is, he used to steal a tiny bit. That is, from people's pockets -- horrors! -- he wouldn't steal, just in his business he would give a weensy drop of false weight." RP, p. 75.)[104]

Very similar is the following 'exoneration' of a vintner who waters his wine:

(145) *Vaser iz gevén in shtetl genúg, un der yid hot gehaltn, az a sakh vayn iz nit gezúnt, un er hot gezórgt, az di goyim un di khsidim, vos veln trinken zayne vayn, zoln zikh kholile nit ónshikern vi di khazeyrim.* ("Water there was aplenty in the town, and the Jew maintained that too much wine wasn't good for you, and was concerned lest the Gentiles and Hasidim who would drink his wines might -- horrors! -- get as drunk as pigs." RP, p. 91.)

Sometimes *kholile* is used ironically though not sarcastically -- that is, there is no malicious intent, only a humorous one. The humor resides in inserting *kholile* into a sentence which expresses a *desirable* state of affairs; i.e. the substitution of a malo-fugitive formula for the expected bono-petitive one:

(146) *Oyb mayn zun volt kholile khásene hobn mir der milyonerke, vos volt ikh take getón?* ("If my son did -- horrors! -- marry that millionaire's daughter, what in the world would I do?")[105]

Often *kholile* constitutes an utterance all by itself. In these cases it functions as an interjection, with a meaning something like *are you kidding? of course not!* . It is used to indicate that what has just been said is so ridiculous or absurd that it is to be rejected out of hand:

(147) *Ikh'l avade geyn, take morgn in der fri. Ikh'l dokh nit esn fun áyere letste. Kholile!* ("Of course I'll leave, tomorrow morning in fact. I certainly won't eat your last crumb. Horrors!" RP, p. 123.)

Most of the time interjectory *kholile* occurs as the answer to a 'silly question,' either one that someone else asks (as in 148), or one that you ask yourself, only to dismiss immediately as absurd (149-152):[106]

(148) *"Vos meynt ir epes, mir veln aykh zháleven tsuker?" "Neyn, kholile! Ikh meyn keyn beyz nit, nor ikh bin a yid, vos ikh hob lib a sakh tsuker."* (" 'What do you think, we're going to begrudge you the sugar?' 'No, horrors! I mean no offense, I'm just a Jew who likes a lot of sugar.' " RP, p. 126.)

(149) *Meynt ir, ikh bin gevorn tsetumlt? Kholile!* ("Do you think I got confused? Horrors no!" RP, p. 101.)

(150) *Fregt men im, "Nu, un ir? Kent ir oykh gut shvimen?" Zogt er, "Shvimen? Kholile! A katshke bin ikh?"* ("So they ask him, 'Well, what about you? Can you also swim well?' And he says, 'Swim? Horrors no! Am I a duck?' ")

(151) *Meynt ir, Beyle vart? Kholile. Zi nemt un est uf nokh a maránts.* ("Do you think that Beyle waits? Horrors no! She takes another orange and gobbles it up." RP, p. 143.)

(152) *Makht der yid: "Krank? Kholile! Úndzere sonim zoln zayn krank! Ikh bin gezúnt!"* ("And the Jew says, 'Sick? Horrors no! May our enemies be sick! I am healthy!' " RP, p. 137.)[107]

More emphatic variants of *kholile* are *khas-ve-kholile* and *kholile-ve-khas*. Also belonging in this group of Hebrew-derived unanalyzable

malo-fugitive expressions is *khas-ve-sholem*.[108] These stronger and
more sonorous formulas are almost always reserved for cases where
genuine danger is involved, and do not lend themselves to ironic
manipulation:

(153) [*Shisn*]*ba der nakht oykh? Vos heyst? Me ken dokh nokh,
khas-ve-sholem, trefn émetsn in oyg!* ("[Shooting] at night too?
What do you mean? You could even, horror of horrors, hit somebody
in the eye!" RP, p. 45.)

(154) *Az es volt, khas-ve-sholem, gevén a sakone, volt dir gelegn
in kop tsu loyfn telegrafirn?* ("If there had been, horror of
horrors, a danger, would it have entered your head to run and send a
telegram?" RP, p. 69.)

(155) *Geyt, vos redt ir? Es ken dokh nokh, khas-ve-sholem, zayn
a tsuzámenshtoys.* ("Come on, what are you talking about? There
could always be, horror of horrors, a crash." RP, p. 133.)

7.3 *Invoking the Aid of a Benevolent God*

(a) *God the Protector.* One of God's guises is Protector of mankind,
the ever-present help in times of trouble. His aid is to be invoked
when someone is embarking on a dangerous or uncertain enterprise:

(156) *Zol dir Got ophitn!* ("May God protect you!")

The expression *Got zol ophitn* 'may God protect' may function as a main
clause with sentential complement:

(157) *Got zol ophitn tsu hobn eyn kind un eyn hemd.* ("May God save
[us] from having one child and one shirt." [Proverb. See YP, p.80.])

When the optative auxiliary *zoln* comes first, the phrase may be parenthetically inserted into a larger sentence, either loosely as in (158),
or more intimately, as in (159):

(158) *A meydl, vos mit ale ofitsirn -- zol aykh Got ophitn!* ("A
girl who -- with all the officers ... may God protect you!" RP,
p. 16.)

(159) [*Ofitsír*] *Zog mir akórsht, tsu vos darf men a biks?* [*Yídish-er zelner*] *Oyf tsum shisn, zol Got ophitn!* ("[Officer] Tell me then, what is a rifle used for? [Jewish soldier] To shoot with, may God protect us!" RP, p. 58.)[109]

A more literary equivalent of *Got zol ophitn* is the Hebrew-derived expression *Got zol shoymer u-matsil zayn* 'may God guard and save us:'

(160) *In a shtot iz gevén a yid, a groyser nogid, nor karg, az Got zol shoymer u-matsil zayn.* ("In a town there was a Jew, a big tycoon, but stingy -- may God guard and save us [from the like]." RP, p. 105.)[110]

(b) *God the Compassionate.* Instead of viewing God as the mighty Protector, one can relate to Him as to a merciful parent, relying on his compassion to keep evil at bay. Apotropaic formulas in this vein contain verbs like *zikh derbáremen* or *rakhmones hobn* 'take pity on' :

(161) *Ay vozhe den? Men vet mikh shikn shisn? Zol zikh Got derbáremen.* ("What are you suggesting? That they'll send me off to the front lines [lit. 'to shoot']? May God have mercy!" RP, p. 60.)

(162) *Ay vos? Tomer vet der daytsh shisn mikh? Oy, zol Got rakhmones hobn!* ("What now? Suppose the German(s) hit me with a shot? Ah, may God take pity!" RP, ibid.)

(c) *God the Deflector.* One more malo-fugitive expression belongs here, even though the name of God is not explicitly mentioned in it. The key idea here is 'forbidding the evil, turning away the evil, deflecting the evil,'[111] and the word used is *oser* 'forbidden, prohibited' (< Heb.):

(163) *Oser mir azá shand!* ("May I be spared such a disgrace!" [lit. 'May such a disgrace be forbidden to me.'])

In colloquial Yiddish, *oser oyb + Clause* ('lit. 'forbidden if + Clause') has come to mean that the action of the clause is so impossible for the speaker to perform that he can safely offer God a kind of wager: if I *could* do such a thing, then You, God, could forbid *good* things from reaching me, i.e. it is so unlikely that I could do it that I don't mind exposing myself to such an evenutality.   English has similar expressions like *I'll be damned if I can figure that out!* Thus,

(164) *Oser oyb ikh veys, vos tut zikh bay im in shtub.* ("I'll be damned if I know what's going on in his house.")

This expression is really a kind of *oath*, very reminiscent of *zol ikh azóy visn fun beyz, vi + Clause* 'may I know about evil the way [I can perform the action of the Clause].' [*See below* 10.2.][112]

7.4 *Appeasing an Awful and Incomprehensible God*

In the preceding section, we have seen God in His more benevolent guises, where He is viewed as a sort of 'good parent' who stands be- tween mankind and the evils of life.   From another standpoint, God himself is the source of all things, including those which appear evil to us because of our limited understanding.   God is also the 'bad parent' (to use psychoanalytical parlance), the one who punishes us, the one who at any moment can inflict terrible calamities on us for reasons we cannot grasp.   This is the God who must be *appeased*, rather than invoked:

(165) *Es iz biter.   Zayn vayb iz im, nit far keyn yidn gedákht, geshtorbn, nebekh a yung vaybl, a mame fun dray kinderlekh, sheyne vi di táybelekh.   Nor itster hot er shoyn, borkhashém, nit mer vi tsvey kinderlekh.   Der zun zayner iz krank gevorn un iz geshtorbn.* ("It's a terrible thing.   His wife -- *may it be unthinkable for all Jews* -- died on him, a young woman, *poor thing,* the mother of three little children, pretty as doves.   But now he already has -- *blessed be the name of the Lord* -- only two little children.   His son got sick and died." RP, p. 104.)

The speaker is recounting a tale of woe, and peppers his narrative with psycho-ostensive formulas: the malo-fugitive *nit far keyn yidn*

gedákht, the malo-recognitive *nebekh*, and then -- rather surprisingly
-- the bono-recognitive *borkhashém* [*see above 3.0*]. In the midst of
telling how one of the poor man's children died right after the death
of the mother, the speaker blesses the name of God. This is the
attitude expressed in the Book of Job 1:21 :

(166) *Adoynóy nosán, ve-Adoynóy lokákh. Yehí shem Adoynóy mevoy-*
rókh. ("The Lord gave, and the Lord hath taken away; blessed be the
name of the Lord.")

The motivation for this humble attitude is quite complex, though one
element in it seems clear: one dare not excessively bemoan one's
fate, because to do so might be to invite an even worse disaster. 'If
you think *that's* bad,' God can always say, 'wait until I show you what
I can do if I really set My mind to it ...' It therefore behooves us
to minimize our woes, in the hope of avoiding even greater 'punishment.'[113] Count your blessings, lest even the little you have be taken
away from you!

(167) *Haleváy vayter nit erger!*[114] ("Would that it get no worse!")

(168) *Beser ken zayn, nor haleváy vayter nit erger!* ("It could be
better, but please don't make it any worse!")

(169) *Kuk aróp, vestu visn vi hoykh du shteyst.* ("Look down and
you'll know how high you stand." YP, p. 90.)[115]

(170) *Men tor nit betn oyf a nayem meylekh.* ("One shouldn't pray
for a new king." YP, p. 92.)[116]

When one of your possessions gets broken or lost, you shouldn't com-
plain, but rather say something like:

(171) *Keyn grésern brokh zoln mir nit hobn!* ("May no worse disaster
strike us!")[117]

When someone complains to you about something relatively trivial, you
would do well to remind him of his place in the scheme of things:

(172) *Keyn grésere tsores zolstu nit hobn!* ("May you never have
worse troubles [than that]!")

When a child comes to you with a scraped knee or cut finger, you may say to him tenderly:

(173)   *Dos vet zikh farheyln biz der khásene!*   ("That will heal before your marriage!")

When a very old person dies, you express sympathy but hasten to add:

(174)   *Keyn yíngere fun im zoln nit shtarbn!*   ("May nobody die younger than him!")

   This awareness of human vulnerability in the face of possible misfortunes to come finds overt linguistic expression in the shape of cautious formulas that one should utter whenever speaking of his *plans for the future.* 'The best-laid plans of mice and men *gang aft agley,'* or as the Yiddish proverb has it:

(175)   *Der mentsh trakht un Got lakht.*   ("Man makes plans and God laughs;" "Man proposes but God disposes.")

The most common of these future-hedges is *im yirtse hashém* (< Heb. 'if the Name wills it'), reduced in rapid speech to something like [mírtsəshem] or [mirčem], regionally [merčem]:

(176)   *In a por vokhn arúm veln mir, im yirtse hashém, shoyn aróyskumen fun dem plonter.*   ("In a couple of weeks, if God wills, we'll already be out of this mess.")

(177)   *Mir zoln zikh zen oyf simkhes, im yirtse hashém ba aykh in der nayer heym.*   ("May we meet again on happy occasions, if God wills it, in your new home.")

(178)   *Dem kúmendikn zumer vel ikh, im yirtse hashém, farbrengen afn breg-yam.*   ("I'll spend next summer at the seashore, if God wills it.")

   Many other parenthetical expressions are available for the job of convincing God that we realize that our future plans are contingent on His continuing to grant us life and good health: *a m'et lebn* 'if I live' (< *az me vet lebn,* lit. 'if one will live');[118] *a m'et lebn efsher* 'if I live, perhaps'; *mir zoln nor zayn gezúnt* 'we should only be healthy; if only our health holds'; *az mir veln lebn un zayn gezúnt* 'if we live and are well'; *az Got vet helfn* 'if God helps,' etc.:

(179) *Morgn, a m'et lebn, vel ikh geyn koyfn hínerfleysh oyf shabes.* ("Tomorrow, if I live, I'll go buy some chicken for the Sabbath.")

At all costs one must avoid rocking the boat.[119]

7.5 *Exorcising the Demons of Misfortune*

Coexisting with the uncompromising monotheism of traditional Jewish life in Eastern Europe was a substratum or overlay of more 'primitive' beliefs that the Jews shared with their Gentile peasant neighbors. These included a rather vague fear of certain evil spirits that had the power to cause illness and even death to their unfortunate victims.[120] They were thought to attack a person through the glance of another. This glance, by means of which the malevolent spirit gained access to its victim, was called the Evil Eye. The person whose glance was responsible (let us call him the *carrier*) need not necessarily have been ill-disposed to the victim. In fact quite the contrary: one of the chief ways the evil spirit could operate was via the *praise* that a carrier conferred on another person. For these spirits were single-mindedly envious of human good fortune. When they would hear someone praised for his health, beauty, or good luck, they would automatically set about trying to turn his happiness into grief. But fortunately, these evil spirits, like their cousins elsewhere in world folk-belief, were none too bright.[121] It was possible to foil them by means of certain simple symbolic actions or magic words, as long as their activities were detected in time.

In a world peopled with such envious spirits, it was only common consideration not to go around praising people indiscriminately, lest one turn oneself into an unwitting 'carrier.' For this reason, Yiddish speakers (especially women) would couch their praises in euphemisms [*see above 7.1*], saying the reverse of what they really meant. This simple device would lull the spirits into blissful dreams of *Schadenfreude*, and no harm would ensue. Thus if a woman saw a particularly beautiful baby, she would never dream of saying:

(180) *(*) Oy, vos far a sheyn éyfele!* ("Oh, what a beautiful baby!")[122]

Rather she would say something like:

(181) *Oy, vos far a míeskayt!* ("Yech, what an ugly thing!"),

probably accompanying her 'reverse praise' by an exorcistic action like turning away and spitting three times. The proud mother would beam in appreciation of this obviously sincere praise.[123] For fending off the Evil Eye was one of the already busy Jewish mother's chief duties:

(182) *Hot dokh der vaybls mame moyre gehát, az ímitser fun di shkheynim zol nit gebn dem kind keyn ayn-hore.* ("But the young wife's mother was afraid that one of the neighbors would give the child an evil-eye." RP, p. 5.)

Instead of using the reverse-praise gambit, another avenue was open to the speaker. That was to go right ahead and give voice to his bono-recognitive sentiments (praises or boasts), but then to append immediately a malo-fugitive or apotropaic formula directed specifically against the Evil Eye. The most common of these is *keyn ayn-hore* or *keyn ayn-hore nit*[124] 'no evil eye' (< Heb. *(ha-)ayin (ha-)raa* 'the evil eye' [absolute] or *eyn ha-ra* 'the eye of evil' [construct]).[125] In rapid speech this tends to be reduced to *keyn aynore*, or even *[kənəhóre]*.[126] A fuller variant is *keyn ayn-hore zol im/ir nit shatn* 'may no evil eye harm him/her.' These formulas may be used either auto-malo-fugitively (when speaking of one's own good fortune) or allo-malo-fugitively (when speaking of somebody else's):

(183) *Ober mir geyt dos, keyn aynore nit, zeyer gut.* ("But for me things are going -- no evil-eye -- very well." RP, p. 124.)

(184) *Háyntiksyor bin ikh gevorn, keyn aynore, akht-un-zíbetsik yor alt.* ("This year I became -- no evil-eye -- 78 years old.")

(185) *Ye, a nogid iz er, keyn aynore zol im nit shatn! Ober er iz*

gevorn a goy.   ("Yes, he certainly is rich, may no evil eye harm him!
But he's become a regular heathen."   RP, p. 44.)

(186) *Men hot zikh gezétst ban tish un me hot zikh gegréyt tsu di
gute maykholim, vorem der yid iz, keyn aynore, gevén a yid a gvir.*
("They sat down at the table and prepared themselves for delicious
food, because the Jew was -- no evil-eye -- a rich man." RP, p.32.)

Note that one need harbor no particular feeling of affection toward
the person one has safeguarded by using the formula to refer to. The
person could be a total stranger, or one may dislike him intensely.
It is as if the speaker were altruistically defending all Jewry, or
all mankind, from the common demonic enemy.

Conversely, if one pointedly omits such a formula, one's ill-will
toward the person involved is obvious even if nothing overtly malo-
petitive is said:

(187) *Un itst fort er arúm in a Kédilek!* ("And now he's driving
around in a Cadillac!")

This is an easy way to wish someone ill by an omission rather than
a commission.[127,128]

Keyn ayn-hore may also appear sarcastically in contexts like the
following:

(188) *Iz ober der fish gevén, keyn ayn-hore, a langer, hot me
aróysgezen dem ek fun unter der kapote.* ("But the fish was -- no
evil-eye -- a long one, so you could see the tail sticking out
from under his kaftan." *L'Chayim*, p. 86.)

The man has just tried to steal the fish, so that its great length
was by no means an advantage to the thief. But the teller of the
joke speaks of the fish as if it were a child whose large size was a
good quality that had to be protected by the formula.

Keyn ayn-hore may be used as an utterance all by itself, e.g. in
response to an inquiry about one's affairs:

(189) *'Nu, vos makht epes ayer zun?' 'Keyn ayn-hore!'* (" 'So
how's your son doing?' 'No evil-eye!' ")

This is understood to mean 'Fine, thank you.' My son is doing so well
that if I *told* you how well, the demons of misfortune would be envious,
so I won't tell you how well, but will exorcise the devils anyway just
in case they should get any funny ideas.

As often in Yiddish, one has the choice between Hebrew- and
Germanic-derived synonyms. Instead of *ayn-hore*, one may refer to
the *beyz oyg* (*beyz eyg* in Litvish dialect) 'evil eye.'[129] This
appears in formulas only in the fuller form *keyn beyz oyg zol im/ir
nit shatn* 'may no evil eye harm him/her.'   Thus one cannot say
(190a), though (190b) is fine:

(190a) **Mayn tokhter, keyn beyz oyg nit, est gut.*

(190b)   *Mayn tokhter, keyn beyz oyg zol ir nit shatn, est gut.*
("My daughter, may no evil eye harm her, eats well.")

Related to the *beyz oyg* is the notion of the *beyze sho* 'evil
hour.'[130] When one is speaking of an unpleasant event that might come
to pass at a certain time in the future, he may signify his malo-
fugitive attitude by the formula *di beyze sho nit* 'may that evil hour
not [come]':

(191) *Efsher kumt undz di shviger tsu gast ibermorgn, di beyze sho
nit.* ("Maybe my mother-in-law is going to visit us the day after
tomorrow, may that evil hour not come!")

Sometimes emergency action is called for to combat the Evil Eye.
Suppose someone has mentioned a horrible thing that might happen, or
bestowed some thoughtless praise without remembering to include any
apotropaic formula. In such cases one can mutter a protective incantation under one's breath, like:

(192) *Zalts dir in di oygn, fefer dir in noz!* ("Salt into your
eyes, and pepper into your nose!")[131]

Or else one can admonish the thoughtless 'carrier' with:

(193) *Bayst zikh op di tsung!* ("Bite off your tongue!")[132]

Suppose some inauspicious sight is seen, such as a cat washing itself on the threshold of a room.   One may say:

(194) *Oyf ale puste felder, oyf ale viste velder!* ("On all the
empty fields, on all the desolate woods [may the misfortune land,
not on us]!")

If none of this seems sufficient, one may spit three times
(*ópshpayen dray mol*),[133] tie a red ribbon onto one's person (*onton
a royt bendl*), overturn a drinking-glass (*íberkern a gloz*), or perform
any of a whole repertoire of similar symbolic actions.[134] (We leave
these as an exorcise for the reader.)

7.6 *The Scapegoat Approach*

One way to deflect evil away from oneself is to offer an alternative victim to the powers of evil: somebody else to take the rap, a
scapegoat.

To see somebody else squirm while one is in no discomfort oneself
is a luxury which occasionally appeals to the most altruistic of men.
As the proverb has it,

(194a) *Oyf yenems tokhes iz gut tsu shmaysn.* ("It's nice to beat
on the other guy's ass.")

On a more cosmic level, the idea of transferring the sins of the
community onto an animal who would then be ritually slaughtered is,
of course, an ancient one in Jewish culture, dating from pre-Biblical
times. It has survived until very recently in the form of the ritual
known as *shlogn kapores* ('beating the atonements'). This ceremony
was performed soon before Yom Kiper, the Day of Atonement, and involved
twirling a live fowl over one's head while reciting certain prayers,
in the hopes that one's own sins would be visited upon the animal.
This hapless bird was known as the *kapore-hindl* or 'scape-fowl.'[135]

By extension, *kapore* came to mean any expiatory punishment or
misfortune, or the victim of such a misfortune.[136] If somebody whose
virtue is open to question suffers some evil, one may say vindictively:

(195) *A sheyne reyne kapore!* ("A fine, pure expiation!"; i.e.
"serves him right!")

More sympathetically one could say:

(196) *Zol dos zayn di kapore far im.* ("May that redeem him [from
an even worse fate].")

But one can go a step further, and wish that somebody else's misfortune
may not benefit *him*, but rather the speaker himself. Thus if somebody
breaks his leg crossing a rickety bridge, you could breathe a sigh of
relief and say:

(197) *Zol dos zayn di kapore far mir!* ("May that be an expiation
for me!")[137]

That is, whenever I have occasion to cross rickety bridges in the
future, may the spirits of misfortune remember that they have already
enjoyed breaking one leg, so they can leave mine alone.

Note that these expressions stop short of actually wishing evil
on others just to escape evil oneself (i.e. they are not actually allo-
malo-petitive in the sense of section 9, *below*). Rather they are an
attempt to utilize the evil that has already befallen somebody else
for one's own malo-fugitive purposes.[138,139]

An altruistic twist to the scapegoat approach is also possible.
You can offer your own misfortune, real or hypothetical, as a gift in
order to save others from evil. This is the strategy of Jesus, and, *mu-
tatis mutandis*, of Jewish mothers. If you are actually suffering some
evil, you can recognize that fact (auto-malo-recognition) and dedicate
it to someone else's good (allo-bono-petition, or allo-malo-fugition).
The expression *ópkumen far NP* 'suffer on NP's behalf' is appropriate
here. If you are gravely ill, you may say:

(198) *Ikh zol shoyn ópkumen far ale mayne kinder.* ("May my suffering be for all my children.")

More frequently, perhaps, you merely ask to assume some hypothetical
burden of evil (a kind of *pro forma* auto-malo-petition), in order to
lighten someone else's misfortune. The commonest formula to use here

is *mir zol zayn far NP* 'may it be so to me on NP's behalf.' Thus if a child falls and scrapes his finger, his mother might say:

(199) *Mir zol zayn far dayn fingerl!* (lit. "May it be so to me on your little finger's behalf," i.e. "I wish it had been my finger instead of yours;" "Would that my finger were hurting instead of yours.")

The object of the preposition *far* is usually either a personal pronoun (as in 200), or a particular body-part belonging to the wishificiary (199, 201):

(200) *Mir zol zayn far dir!* ("I wish it were me instead of you!")

(201) *Mir zol zayn far dayn képele / dayne béyndelekh!* ("If only *I* could suffer instead of your little head/your little bones.")

The expression *oyf mir di aveyre* 'may the sin be upon *me* [instead of you]' is similar psychosemantically to the preceding, but used in quite different contexts. This is what you say when you are trying to convince someone that it would be all right to perform a certain action, that he need have no moral qualms about it. Thus if you are tempting someone who is nominally on a diet to go ahead and have a second piece of cake you could say:

(202) *Vos shemstu zikh? Nem nokh a shtíkele! Oyf mir di aveyre!* ("Why be bashful? Take another little piece! May the sin be on me!")

Here, obviously, the self-sacrifice involved is purely hypothetical.

They tell a story about a mother who insisted that her son, a husky truck-driver, wear a sweater to work one day, lest he catch cold. When he refused, she ran outdoors and lay down in the path of the front wheels of the truck, uttering the immortal words:

(203) *For mir iber mitn trok, oyb du trogst nit keyn sveter!* ("Run me over with your truck if you won't wear a sweater!")[140]

Truly it is said:

(204) *In vaser un fayer volt zi gelofn far ir kind.* ("She would
run through water and fire for her child.")[141]

8.0 PSYCHO-OSTENSIVES RELATING TO THE DEAD

Yiddish shares with many other languages the habit of using set
formulas to accompany the mention of a dead person in conversation.
English has relatively few such expressions (*May he rest in peace* and
God rest his soul are about the only ones now current in the U.S.), and
they are not much used by the average speaker. Yiddish has more of
them, and they are so frequently used that they are practically obligatory whenever a dead person's name comes up. They reflect a variety
of psychic attitudes toward the dead on the part of the speaker.

(a) *Blessing the dead.* In the usual case, one blesses the name of
the dead person.[142] We may call the attitude this reflects *mortuo-
bono-petitive.* The living do not know what constitutes a 'good' for
the dead, though we assume that what they want and need most is *rest*
or *peace*, and an honored place in the memory of the living. The
strictly bono-petitive formulas are all derived from Hebrew. The
holy language is more suitable than the vernacular for this solemn
purpose.

The most common mortuo-bono-petitive formula is *olevasholem*
(< Ashkenazic Heb. *olov ha-sholoym,* mod. Israeli *alav ha-shalom* 'unto
him be peace'). Since the first word *olov* 'unto him' contains an
incorporated masculine object *-ov* 'him,' this is strictly speaking
usable only for dead males. The feminine counterpart 'unto her' is
oleho in Ashkenazic Hebrew, yielding the expression *oleho ha-sholoym.*
This is not easily pronounceable in Yiddish, where the whole expression
is treated as a single word with strong primary stress on the penult
-sho-, so that the first few syllables get weak stress. This has
led to haplology of the two successive *-ho-/-ha-* syllables, yielding
olehasholem, or even *olesholem.* The phonological similarity between
this feminine formula and the corresponding masculine one has led to a

breakdown of the distinction for many speakers, so that *olevasholem* can be used indiscriminately for a dead man or woman. When more than one dead person is referred to, the correct formula to use is *aleyem-hasholem* 'unto them peace.' But even this distinction is disappearing, and *olevasholem* bids fair to become an invariant expression usable with masculine or feminine, singular or plural:

(205) *Mayn tate un mame, olevasholem/aleyem-hasholem, hobn dos nebekh nisht derlébt tsu zen.* ("My father and mother, unto them peace, didn't, unfortunately, live to see that.")

(206) *Hob ikh zikh teykef gevólt getn. Zogt tsu mir der tate mayner, olevasholem, az es iz a bizoyen far der velt.* ("So I wanted to get divorced right away. [But] my father, peace unto him, told me it would be a public disgrace." RP, p. 23.)

(207) *In hundert-un-tsvantsik yor arúm volt ikh gevélt lign nebn Reb Dovid Sorele's, olevasholem.* ("In 120 years from now I'd like to lie next to Reb Dovid, Sorele's son, unto him peace." RP, p. 171.)[143]

More elegant formulas, usable when the dead person was a figure of some standing or of conspicuous virtue, are *zikhroyne livrokhe* 'may his memory be a blessing,' and *skhusoy yogeyn oleynu* 'may his merit protect us,' both from Hebrew.

So irrepressible is Yiddish humor that even these necrological formulas may be used for comic effect:

(208) *Mir hobn étlekhe doktoyrim, nor der bester fun zey iz der dokter Grinshteyn -- a táyerer dokter! Er hot gehéylt di shenste balabatim fun shtetl mit di faynste nemen: Reb Dóvidl Íserles, olevasholem; Reb Yánkele Rápoport, zikhroyne livrokhe; Reb Yitskhok Spektor, skhusoy yogeyn oleynu -- táyere nemen!* ("We have several doctors, but the best of them is Dr. Greenstein -- a wonderful doctor! He has treated the most distinguished householders of our town, with the finest names: Mr. D. I., unto him peace; Mr. Y. P., may his memory be a blessing; Mr. Y. S., may his merit protect us -- wonderful names!" RP, p. 138.)

Other mortuo-bono-petitive expressions, usable as independent utterances as well as parenthetically, include:

(209) *Zol er/zi lign in zayn/ir ru.*   ("May he/she lie in his/her rest.")[144]

(210) *Zol er/zi hobn a likhtikn gan-eydn.*   ("May he/she have a radiant paradise.")[145,146]

(b) *Exploiting the dead.*   Occasionally when a dead person is mentioned it is with the thought that he might somehow still provide some benefit for the living by interceding with God on our behalf.   We may call formulaic expressions that express this attitude *vivo-bono-petitive*. They include *skhusoy yogeyn oleynu* 'may his merit be a shield for us' [*mentioned in the previous section*],[147] and also the following:

(211a) *Zol er zayn a guter beter far undz.*

(211b) *Zol zi zayn a gute beterin far undz.*
("May he/she be a good supplicant on our behalf.")[148]

(c) *Fearing the dead.*   In all cultures, perhaps, the living have feared the dead at some level of consciousness.   The roots of this feeling are not hard to trace.   The living possess a commodity, life, which the dead no longer have.   Therefore it is only natural to imagine that the dead must envy the living; since misery loves company, wouldn't the dead like to see the living dead too?[149]   This is the attitude behind the brutal Latin inscription formerly in vogue on tombstones: *Sum quod eris* 'I am what thou shalt be.'

In Yiddish, this visceral fear sometimes manifests itself in the form of vivo-malo-fugitive or vivo-bono-petitive formulas attached to the name of a dead person.   These are designed to insure that the speaker and hearer, or some living third person mentioned in the same breath as the dead person, will not be enticed to die before their time by the blandishments of the dead.   The formula is usually of the following shape:

(212)
$$\left\{\begin{array}{l} undz \\ dir/aykh \\ im/ir/Velvlen \end{array}\right\} \; + \; tsu \; + \; \left\{\begin{array}{l} lange \\ l\acute{e}ngere \end{array}\right\} \; + \; yor(n).$$

In the first slot appears the NP referring to the living person who is being protected by the formula, either a first person plural pronoun (*undz* 'us'), a second person pronoun (*dir* or *aykh*), or a third person pronoun or noun (*im* 'him,' *ir* 'her,' *Velvlen* 'to Velvel,' *ayer zun* 'your son,' etc.). All these NP's must be in the dative case. Note that the first person singular pronoun is inappropriate here, since it would be intolerably selfish to protect oneself but not one's listener:

(212a)   *(*) Mir tsu lange yor.*

After the proposition *tsu* 'to, toward' comes the plural adjective meaning 'long,' either in the simplex or comparative form (*lange* 'long,' *léngere* 'longer'), followed by the word for 'years,' treated either as a count noun (*yorn*) or a mass noun (*yor*). The whole expression means something like 'for us toward long(er) years,' i.e. 'may the living go on living a long time.' Thus,

(213) *Un beyde mekhutonim zaynen shoyn haynt, aykh tsu lange yorn, oyf der béserer velt.* ("And both sets of in-laws are now already -- may *you* live long years -- in the better world." RP, p. 105.)

(214) *Efsher gedenkstu Shmerln? Er iz gevén in zélbikn klas mit dayn zun, im tsu léngere yor.* ("Maybe you remember Shmerl? He was in the same class as your son, may *he* live longer years.")

(215) *Azóy flegt es kokhn mayn shviger, undz tsu lange yor.* ("That's how my mother-in-law used to cook it -- may *we* live long years.")

(d) *Speaking ill of the dead.* In general one tries to speak well of the dead in Yiddish, as in other languages: *De mortuis nil nisi bonum.* To speak ill of the dead might be to invite reprisals from beyond the tomb [*preceding section*]. If one finds himself making a critical remark about a dead person, he would normally add an apologetic or *palliative* formula like *zol er mir moykhl zayn* 'may he forgive me (for saying so)':

(216) *Mayn feter Shloyme iz gevén, zol er mir moykhl zayn, epes a shnorer.* ("My uncle Shloyme was -- may he forgive me -- something of a mooch.")[150]

Occasionally, however, the dead person whose name is mentioned was a real enemy, and the speaker's hostility toward him is unabated and unmollified after his death. In these cases, one does not fear reprisals, and there is a rich store of *mortuo-malo-petitive* expressions at one's disposal:

(217) *Zol er lign in drerd!* ("May he rot [lit.'lie'] in hell!")

(218) *Di erd zol im aróysvarfn!* ("May the earth throw him out!")

(219) *Zol er fartsn in zamd!* ("May he fart in the sand!")[151]

In some ways the strongest of these expressions are those which express the wish that the dead person's memory should be forever wiped out from the consciousness of the living. These terrible formulas are mostly reserved for heinous figures of historical significance, like Hitler (whose names paradoxically will never die). One may use either the Hebrew-derived expression *yimákh shemóy* 'may his name be erased!' or the Germanic *zol er óysgemekt vern* 'may he be erased!'[152]

On this hostile note, we continue to our discussion of *allo-malo-petitive* expressions in general.

9.0 ALLO-MALO-PETITION: CURSES!

It sometimes happens that people 'have words with' each other in Yiddish. One word for having-words-with is *dúrkhvertlen zikh* 'exchange angry words' (lit. 'to word through with each other' < *vort* 'word' or *vertl* 'epigram, proverb, flavorful expression').[153] Stronger verbs, implying real abusiveness and hostility, are *shiltn zikh* and *zidlen zikh:*[154]

(220) *Tsvey yidn hobn zikh amól tsekrígt, eyner dem andern gezídlt,*
biz eyner iz gevorn mole-kas ...   ("Once two Jews were quarreling
with each other, one cursing the other, until one of them got really
mad ..." RP, p. 36.)

At its simplest level, Yiddish verbal abuse takes the form of
cusswords or epithets (*zídlverter*) that the speaker applies to his
antagonist. These are unlimited in number, since the speaker has the
whole arsenal of Germanic, Hebrew, and Slavic insults at his disposal,
along with many original Yiddish *trouvailles*. There is little point
in attempting to enumerate them here, entertaining as that would be.[155]

Instead of individual lexical items like *paskudnyák* 'scoundrel'
or *hultáy* 'debauchee, libertine,' what we are concerned with here is
the ritualized curse, or *klole* (< Heb.): petitive expressions that
call down misfortune, disease, or death on their intended victims.
Needless to say, the malo-petitioner would often be appalled if the
dire eventuality actually came to pass. We English speakers would not
like it if people obligingly expired every time we said *Drop dead!* to
them. *Kloles* are rather to be viewed as the overt linguistic manifestation of a momentary psychic state: hostility. Note that *klole* is
a meta-term, and is not usable as a curse itself. It is nonsense to
say:

(221) **A klole oyf dir!* ("A curse on you!")

In the following discussion the key words in section 9.1 have
already been encountered in other psycho-ostensive contexts, while
those in 9.2ff comprise material that only appears in curses.

9.1 *Expressions Already Encountered in Other Psycho-Ostensive Contexts*

(a) *Klog* and *brokh*. We have seen [*4.0 above*] how *klog* 'lament' and
brokh 'disaster' may be used auto-malo-recognitively with a first-
person object: *a klog/brokh tsu mir!* ("Woe is me!"). When the object is non-first person, these expressions become curses (i.e. the
auto- becomes allo-, and the recognitive becomes petitive). Usually

they are of the form

  a klog/brokh tsu NP   '[may] a lament/disaster [come] to NP.'

See examples (22) and (23) above, and also:

  (222) *Er hot bay mir óysgenart mayne fuftsik dolar, a klog/brokh tsu im!* ("He cheated me out of my fifty dollars, damn him!")

These expressions may constitute utterances by themselves, or may be used parenthetically, as in the examples. A more emphatic variant is:

  (223) *A klog/brokh zol NP xapn!* ("May a lament/disaster grab NP!")

More specific and elaborate is the independent utterance:

  (224) *Zolstu geyn mit a klog iber di hayzer!* ("May you go with a lament from door to door [begging]!")[156]

    While on the subject of wishing someone poverty, we may mention the following curse, which is appropriate as a counter-thrust to some-one who envies your good fortune:

  (225) *Ver 's fargínt mir nit zol aléyn nit hobn.* ("May he who be-grudges me not have it himself!")[157]

(b) *Wishes for a bad year.* We have already [5.0d above] noted the importance of the concept of a year's run of luck in Jewish culture. Wishing someone a bad year is one of the most frequent malo-petitive gambits in Yiddish.

    The phrase *shvarts yor* 'black year, year of misfortune' is often used as an *expletive* rather than a real curse: i.e. as an impersonal expression of anger or displeasure, not directed at any individual in particular. To say *a shavarts yor!* in this spirit is equivalent to saying *God damn it all!* in English. More emphatic is *shvarts blutiks yor* (lit. 'black, bloody year'):

  (226) *Shvarts blutiks yor! Ir gloybt mir nit?* ("God damn it all to hell! Don't you believe me?" RP, p. 129.)

Still in the expletive category are the expressions *in ale shvartse yorn* and *tsu al di shvartse yor* (lit. 'into all years of misfortune'):[158]

(227) *In ale shvartse yorn! Zi hot mir gegebn a mílkhikn meser, hot zi mir gegebn!* ("Damn it all! She gave me a dairy knife, she did!" RP, p. 95.)[159]

Shvarts yor is sometimes used to mean the 'cause of a misfortune,' or simply 'a nuisance':

(228) *Vos iz dos far a shvarts yor? Vos darf ikh dem kelev?* ("What kind of black year is this? What do I need this mutt for?" RP, p.56.)

In direct address, *shvarts yor* may appear in imperative sentences, like English *Go to hell!*:[160]

(229) *Geyt in ale shvartse yorn! Ikh gib keyn nedoves nit.* ("Go to hell! I never give charity." RP, p. 130.)

Most serious of all is the actual malo-petition

a shvarts/fintster yor oyf + NP 'a black/dark year on NP':

(230) *A shvarts yor oyf ir, a gantsn tog hot zi mir geháhkt a tshaynik vegn kléynikaytn!* ("A black year on her, all day long she chewed my ear off with trivia!")[161]

We have already mentioned in passing [*5.0d above*] the malo-petitive use of the construction *azá yor oyf NP, vi + Clause* 'may NP have such a year as Clause.' Cf. sentence (60) and also:

(231) *Azá yor oyf im, vi er hot mir farríkht di mashín.* ("May he have such a year as the way he fixed my car!")

That is, he did such a rotten job fixing my car that I wish him a year's luck that is equally rotten. This construction is an example of the distinctively Yiddish type of malediction that I call *comparative curses* [*below 9.5*].

Instead of *shvarts yor*, one sometimes uses the euphemism *der guter yor* 'the good year' [*see next section*].

(c) *Visn 'to know (of evil)'.* We have already met the verb *visn* 'know' in a malo-fugitive context [*above 7.1*]. The phrase *me zol nit visn* 'one should not know [of such evil things]' is a common apotropaic formula.

Alternatively, one may use this verb in curses, expressing the wish that the maleficiary may 'know' (i.e. experience) some evil. In these formulas the auxiliary verb *zoln* does not usually appear; rather *visn* itself is used in an optative sense.

One of the commonest of these phrases involves the word *klog* [*(a) above*]: *klog veys + NP* 'may a lament be known to NP.' Thus:

(232) *Mayn shviger, klog veys ir, hot a beyze tsung.* ("My mother-in-law, may a lament be known to her, has a wicked tongue.")

Often that which one wishes the maleficiary to 'know' is a bad year [*(c) above*], generally in the euphemistic guise of *a gut yor,* or *der guter yor* 'the good year':[162]

(233) *Der guter yor veys im, dem galekh!* ("May the 'good year' be known to him, that priest!" RP, p. 149.)

In one interesting construction, *visn* and *der guter yor* appear together with an interrogative pronoun (*vi* 'how,' *vu* 'where,' *far vos* 'why,' etc.) as an *indefinite* substitute for an adverbial clause. This is very similar to English expressions like 'however the hell,' 'wherever the hell,' etc.:

(234) *Dos hobn zey óysgelernt ergets vu fun a bukh, tsi veys zey der guter yor vu.* ("That they learned someplace from a book, or the-devil-knows-where." [lit. "...or wherever the 'good year' may be known to them."])

The concept of 'knowing a good year' also appears in a neatly turned *comparative curse* [*9.5 below*]:

(235) *Zol ikh azóy visn fun im, un er fun a gut yor.* ("May I know from him the way he should know from a good year."; i.e. "May I have as little to do with him as he experiences good luck in the coming year."; i.e. "May my contact with him be as rare as his contact with good luck this year.").

(d) *Oyf NP gezógt gevorn* *'May it be said of NP'*. This versatile expression has already been found both in bono-petitive [5.0c] and malo-fugitive [7.1] contexts. When the NP refers to someone who is the object of the speaker's hostility (e.g. *mayne sonim* 'my enemies,' *der tsar* 'the czar,' etc.), the phrase becomes malo-petitive:

(236) *'S iz gevén a mies háyzkele, oyf mayne sonim gezógt gevorn.* ("It was an ugly little hut, may it be said of my enemies," i.e. so ugly that I might wish my enemies to have such a one.)[163]

We now proceed to consider expressions that are only used with malo-petitive purport.

9.2 *Curses With* ruekh *'Ghost, Evil Spirit'*

The word *ruekh* (< Heb.; pl. *rukhes*) 'ill wind, ghost, demon' is used in a variety of curses. Sometimes these are of the impersonal, expletive type:

(237) *Tsu ale (shvartse) rukhes!* ("To the devil with it! [lit. 'to all (black) spirits!']")

In direct curses, the *ruekh* may be invited to seize the maleficiary from without (*khapt NP der ruekh* 'may the spirit seize NP!'), or to enter inside the maleficiary and take possession of him from within[164] (*a ruekh in NP [aráyn]* 'may a spirit enter into NP'). In this latter case, the speaker often selects the father or paternal grandfather of the addressee as maleficiary:[165]

(238) *A ruekh in dayn tatn aráyn!* ("May a demon enter into your father!")[166]

(239) *A ruekh in dayn tatns tatn aráyn!* ("May a demon enter into your father's father!")

(239) is a more violent curse than (238), probably simply because of its greater sonority. Note that it sounds funny to use the monomorphemic *zeyde* 'grandfather' instead of *tatns tate* 'father's father':

(240) *(*) A ruekh in dayn zeydn aráyn!*

Expressions like (239) are the basis for a general term for violent
cursing, *shiltn in tatns tatn* 'to curse unto someone's father's father
curse unto the third generation back.' As in the verse in the humorou
song *Vozhe Vilstu, Mayn Tayer Kind?* 'What would you like [for a hus-
band], my dear child?':

(241) *A shnayder-yingl neyt khalatn*
       Un shilt zayn vayb in tatns tatn.
("A tailor-boy sews up robes / And curses his wife's father's
father.")

9.3 *Calling Down Disease*

One of the most richly productive malo-petitive categories com-
prises expressions which invoke an illness or disease on the maleficiary. It will be convenient to use certain abbreviations to facilitate
the discussion. Let us symbolize the illness or disease by D , the
maleficiary by M , and the particular body-part or organ to be affected by the affliction as O . Practically any disease or body-part
will serve the purpose, though every malo-petitively inclined Yiddish-
speaker has his own stock of favorites which he will tend to use more
often than others.

The commonest members of the class D are general terms like
krenk 'illness;' *veytik* 'pain;' *make* 'plague, scourge, abscess;' *fayer*
'fire, burning pain;' *shtekhenish* 'stabbing, shooting pain,' and names
for a few specific diseases that are especially dreaded in traditional
Jewish culture, like *kholerye* 'cholera'[167] and *kadokhes* 'ague, malaria.'[168,169]

The most-favored members of the class O are *kop* (but never the
diminutive *kepl* or *képele*!), *boykh* 'belly,' *rukn* 'back,' *di yasles*
'the gums,' *di zaytn* 'the sides,' *di pleytses* 'the shoulders, the
back,' *di kishkes* 'the intestines,' *di beyner* 'the bones,' etc.

These curses, which may all be used either as independent utterances or parenthetically, fall into a few general syntactic patterns:

(a) $zol + M + V_d$

(242) *Zol zi geshvoln vern vi a barg!* ("May she swell up like a mountain!")

(243) *Zol er dos nor óyskrenken!* ("May he only pay the price for it in sickness!")

[(243) is said of someone whom the speaker feels to have acquired something by unfair means.]

(b) $a + D + zol + M + V_{enc}$, or $zol + M + V_{enc} + D$

where V_{enc} symbolizes a 'verb of encountering (illness),' such as *trefn* 'meet with,' *khapn* 'seize with, be seized by,' *varfn in* 'throw into, be thrown into,' etc.

(244) *A fayer zol ir trefn vi zi redt!* ("May a fiery pain meet her, the way she talks!", i.e. "I would rather see a fire consume her than listen to her talk." RP, p. 13.)

(245) *A kholerye zol im khapn!* ("May the cholera seize him!")

(246) *Zol im varfn in kadokhes!* ("May he be thrown into an ague!" RP, p. 116.)

(c) $a + D + M_{dat} + in + O$ / $a + D + in + M_{gen} + O$ /
$a + D + zol + M_{dat} + aráyn + in + O$

In illness-curses of this type, the organ of one's choice is specified. The maleficiary usually appears in the dative case, with no possessive adjective before the organ; alternatively the maleficiary may be in the genitive, directly before O. Either no verb is used, or else the auxiliary *zoln* appears in conjunction with the pro-verb *aráyn* '(go) into':

(247) *A gezunte kholerye dir in boykh!* ("A healthy cholera into your belly!" RP, p. 162.)

(248) *A make aykh in di beyner!* ("A plague on all your bones!" RP, p. 124.)

(249) *A kholerye dir in di beyner, a make dir in boykh, a ruekh in dayn tatns tatn aráyn!* ("A cholera to your bones, a plague to your belly, a demon into your father's father!" RP, p. 124.)

(250) *A veytik in mayne sonims kep!* ("A pain into my enemies' heads!")

(251) *A krenk zol zey aráyn in di zaytn!* ("May a disease enter int their sides!")

More imaginative variations on these themes are readily found:

(252) *Vos es hot zikh mir gekholemt di nakht un letste nakht, zol zikh óyslozn tsu dayn kop un layb un lebn!* ("May my nightmares ['what I dreamt about'] of the last two nights let themselves loose onto your head and body and life!" RP, p. 107.)

9.4   *Calling Down Death*

Most serious of all curses are those where the maleficiary's death is called for.

Among the simplest are those consisting of the optative auxiliary *zoln* plus an intransitive verb of dying:

(253) *Péygern zol er! / Zol er péygern!* ("May he die like a dog!")[170]

(254) *Platsn zol er! / Zol er platsn!* ("May he explode!")

Note that the usual word for 'die,' *shtarbn*, is avoided in these curses. It is intolerably direct and blunt to say right out:

(254a) *(*) Shtarbn zol er!*

Such a bare-faced expression is so 'dangerous' that it might boomerang right back onto the malo-petitioner.

Many death-curses make mention of the final resting-place of humanity, *di erd* 'the earth':

(255) *Ir meynt dem prezidentn? Der hultáy, di erd zol im nit trogn Er voynt vayter, nebn der post.* ("Do you mean the president [of the

congregation]? The whoremaster, may the earth not carry him? He
lives further on, near the post-office." RP. p. 116.)

The prepositional phrase *in der erd* 'in the earth,' usually syncopated
into *in drerd*, is frequent in curses with a meaning much like English
'in hell' or 'to hell':

(256) *Zol er geyn/lign in drerd!* ("May he go to/lie in hell!")

(257) *In drerd mitn kop!* ("Into hell with [his] head!")

(258) *In drerd mit di beyner!* ("Into hell with [his] bones!")

As mentioned above [*5.0, sentence (41)*], *in drerd* or *in drerd aráyn*
may be postposed to clauses as a tag indicating the hostility of the
speaker toward the person mentioned in the clause:

(259) *Er iz a shtik gornisht, in drerd aráyn!* ("He's a real nothing
[lit. 'a piece of nothing'], into hell [with him]!")

(260) *Er vet oykh forn mit undz tsum yaríd, in drerd!* ("He's going
with us to the fair too, to hell [with him]!")

All these curses may be used directly to the second person, with the
imperative of *geyn* 'go':

(261) *Gey (mir) in der erd!* ("Go to hell!"),[171]

(262) *Gey in drerd mit di beyner!* ("Go to hell with your bones!"),

etc.

Often the malo-petitioner wishes to be more vivid, and mentions
a particular mode of violent death that he envisions for his victim.
Such expressions usually consist of *zoln* plus the passive participle
of a transitive verb of killing:[172]

$$zol + M + V_{kill} + vern \quad / \quad V_{kill} + zol + M + vern$$

'may M be V_{kill}'ed!'. (The variant with the main verb coming first
is the more emphatic one.) The verbs of killing constitute an open
class, including such typical members as *hárgenen* 'to murder,'
shisn 'shoot,' *dershtikn* 'choke, suffocate,' *dervergn/dervargn*
'strangle,' *dertrunken* 'drown,' *óysmekn* 'wipe out,' *dershtekhn*

'stab,' *farbrenen* 'burn,' *áynzinken* 'sink, submerge,' etc.:

(263) *Mayn man, zol er geshosn vern, hot nekhtn óngevorn a sakh gelt.* ("My husband, may he be shot, lost a lot of money yesterday.")

(264) *Áyngezunken zol er vern, der balakhsanye!* ("May he be submerged, the innkeeper!" RP, p. 145.)

(265) *Oy, zol er nor dervorgn vern, der ganev!* ("Ah, may he only be strangled, the thief!")

These expressions may all be used directly to the second person, with the imperative of *vern* plus the past participle of the main verb:

(266) *Ver geharget!* ("Be murdered!")

(267) *Ver dershtikt!* ("Be choked!"), etc.

An unlimited number of other curses may be created by using a clause with *zoln* that describes a death-dealing accident or disaster:

(268) *A fayer zol im óntsindn!* ("May a fire ignite him!"),

(269) *A traktor zol im íberforn!* ("May a tractor run him over!"), etc.[173]

If one wishes to be more indirect, he can use the rhetorical question *darf er lebn?* 'must he live?' as a parenthetical death-curse:

(270) *Mayn vayb -- darf zi lebn? -- hot dos im avékgegebn umzist.* ("My wife -- must she live? -- gave it away to him for nothing.")

Another way of avoiding a direct mention of death in a curse is to say:

(271) *A nomen nokh dir/im!* ("A name after you/him!")

This refers to the Ashkenazic Jewish custom of naming children only after dead persons. Everyone wants the honor of eventually having someone named for him. But by outright wishing that someone else may have a namesake, one is *ipso facto* wishing for his immediate death. Similarly, one may say with mock piety:

(272) *Got zol dir/im nor gebn a naye neshome!* ("May God only give you/him a new soul!")

This is an oblique way of saying that you hope the maleficiary's
present soul will soon be given back to its Maker.

The following indirect death-curse is set up in a quasi-syllogistic way. Two premises are given, then the listener is invited to draw
his own conclusion:

(273) *Ven eyner fun undz vet shtarbn, vel ikh forn keyn Erets-
Yisroel.* ("If one of us dies, then *I'll* be the one to travel to
Israel.")[174]

A particularly nasty curse that still manages to avoid a direct
mention of death is:

(274) *Zol im shtinken fun kop/haldz!* ("May it stink from his head/
neck!", i.e. may his head or neck decompose.)

Finally, we may mention death-curses which wear a momentarily
deceptive bono-petitive garb; that is, which start out as life-wishes,
but are given a malicious twist at the end. These include such gems
as the following:

(275) *Zol er lebn -- ober nit lang.* ("May he live -- but not
long.")

(276) *Zol er beser lebn -- un mutshn zikh.* ("Rather let him live --
and suffer.")

(277) *Zol er lebn biz hundert-un-tsvantsik yor -- on a kop.* ("May
he live to be 120 -- without a head.")

(278) *Zol er lebn biz hundert-un-tsvantsik yor -- mit a híltsernem
kop un glézerne oygn.* ("May he live to be 120 -- with a wooden head
and glassy eyes.")   [*See above, note 49.*]

9.5 *Attenuated Curses*

The apparent virulence of Yiddish cursing is often softened by
euphemism, humor, or virtuoso eloquence.

We have already had occasion to mention such lexical euphemisms as *der guter yor* 'good year' for *shvarts yor* 'black year,' or *gut oyg* 'good eye' for *beyz oyg* 'evil eye.' Another sort of euphemistic device consists simply in negating the verb of the curse. This is the ancient rhetorical ploy typified by Marc Antony's remark, 'I do not say that Caesar was ambitious.' (*Julius Caesar,* Act III, Scene 2). I am told that my great-grandmother, a gentle woman, once caught her cat stealing the family's chicken from on top of the *zalts-bret* or 'salting board,' at which she exclaimed furiously:

(279) *Oy, a veytik in dir nit!* ("Oh, may a pain not enter you!")[175]

The speaker thus succeeds in letting off steam, while avoiding the morally questionable act of cursing.

Yiddish curses are often given a humorous twist, which serves to blunt their effect -- one cannot easily laugh and be bitterly malopetitive at the same time:

(280) *A ziser toyt zol er hobn -- a trok mit tsuker zol im iberforn!* ("May he have a sweet death -- run over by a sugar-truck!")

(281) *Zol er vaksn vi a tsibele/burik -- mitn kop in der erd!* ("May he grow like an onion/a beet -- with his head in the ground!")[176]

Of a hypocritically pious Gentile one might sneer:

(282) *Mitn kop in drerd un di fis in kloyster!* ("With his head in the ground and his feet in the church!")

Also in this humorous category are imperative sentences where the speaker urges his antagonist to perform some *humiliating action* (cf. English 'go jump in the lake,' 'go fly a kite,' etc.):

(283) *Gey kakn afn yam!* ("Go take a crap in the sea!")[177]

(284) *Kak zikh oys!* ("Take a crap for yourself!")[178]

(285) *Kush mir in tokhes!* ("Kiss my ass!")[179]

(286) *Kush a bern untern fartekh!* ("Kiss a bear under his apron!" RP, p. 86.)

The most subtle way to defuse curses of their malice is to combine
humor with syntactic elegance. One particularly well-developed genre
is the *comparative curse.* A comparative curse consists of two clauses,
one of which contains optative *zoln* and usually the comparative adverb
azóy 'so; in this way.' This *zoln*-clause expresses the wish that the
maleficiary may experience something or other. This is then compared
to the event or state described in the other clause, which is often
introduced by the comparative conjunction *vi* 'as.' A skillful speaker
can create varied humorous effects, according to how he manipulates
the desirability -- the good/evil dynamics -- of the events mentioned
in the two clauses. In the most straightforward case, the events of
both clauses are undesirable:

zol + M + azóy + BAD THING, vi + BAD THING.

Thus, suppose somebody has made you a present of a fountain-pen, which
you accept, only to find that it leaks terribly, so that every time
you use it you befoul your person. In exasperation you may curse the
giver:

(287) *Oy, zol im nor azóy rinen fun noz, vi 's rint mir fun der
kvalpen!* ("Oh, may his nose only leak on him the way this fountain-
pen leaks on me!")[180]

Less imaginative, but illustrating the same technique[181], is this
sentence describing the sinking of a milkman's horse and wagon through
the thin ice of a frozen river:

(288) *Meyle, vos es iz gevorn fun vogn un fun ferdl un fun der
milkh, zol dos vern mit sone-yisroel!* ("Well, anyway, what became
of the wagon and the horse and the milk should only happen to the
enemies of Israel!" RP, p. 92.)

Psycho-dynamically more complicated, and thus perhaps more funny,
are comparative curses where the event of the *zoln*-clause is *desirable,*
while that of the *vi*-clause is undesirable:

zol + M + azóy + GOOD THING, vi + BAD THING.

The meaning here is sarcastic: may the 'good' things that happen to my

maleficiary be like everybody else's bad things. A classic example is
the story about the czar's progress through a *shtetl*. All the towns-
people, Jews and Gentiles alike, have been mobilized to do him honor,
and have been instructed to stand at the side of the road and shout
'Hurrah!' as he passes:

> (289) *Dortn iz geshtanen eyne a kranke yídene, oykh kukn afn keyser.*
> *Shrayt zi: "Hura, hu-ra! ... Oy, zol er azóy hobn koyekh tsu lebn,*
> *vi ikh hob koyekh tsu shrayen! ... Hu-ra!"* ("There was a certain
> sick Jewish woman standing there, also to have a look at the king.
> Cried she: 'Hooray, hoo-ray! Ah, may he have such strength to live
> as I have strength to shout! ... Hoo-ray!' " RP, p. 58.)

Also in this category is sentence (235) cited above [*9.1c*]:

> (235) *Zol ikh azóy visn fun im, un er fun a gut yor.* ("May I know
> from him the way he should know from a good year.")

We shall presently see that this same 'comparative' syntactic
pattern is the one which must be used for swearing oaths [*below
10.0*].[182]

The Yiddish curse reaches its full flower in the form of set
pieces that are meant to be recited by raconteurs -- elaborate jokes
which revolve entirely around malo-petitive formulas. Consider the
'Agrarian Controversy.'[183] A man is assuring his friend that he gets
along beautifully with his wife, except for one thing:

> (290) *"...Mir krign zikh iber der agrárfrage, ober in ándere zakhn*
> *lebn mir gut." "Vos heyst, ir krigt zikh iber der agrárfrage? Vos*
> *hot ir tsu ton mit der agrárfrage?" Entfert yener: "Farshtéyt ir*
> *mikh -- ikh zog, zi zol lign in der erd, un zi zogt, az ikh zol lign*
> *in der erd."* (" 'We have arguments about the Agrarian Controversy,
> but in other matters we get along fine.' 'What do you mean, you
> have arguments about the Agrarian Controversy? What do you have to
> do with the Agrarian Controversy?' The other answers, 'Don't you
> understand -- I say that *she* should lie in the earth, and she says
> that *I* should lie in the earth.' " RP, p. 13.) [For the curse
> *lign in d(e)rerd*, see above, *9.4.*]

Or take the straight-faced exegesis of the Scriptural phrase *tizal katal imrosi* 'my speech shall distil as the dew' [*Deut. 32:2*]:

(291) *Ir hot gehért dem taytsh fun "tizal katal imrosi?" Vel ikh aykh zogn: tizal -- zol geshvoln vern; katal -- vi a barg; imrosi -- mayn shviger. Vet ir dokh fregn, far vos iz tizal "zol geshvoln vern?" Vos den zol mayn shviger, az nit geshvoln vern? Vet ir dokh vayter fregn, far vos epes katal "vi a barg?" Oyb shoyn ye geshvoln vern, zol zi geshvoln vern vi vos? Vi a barne? Avade vi a barg! Ay vos? Ir vet fregn, far vos iz imrosi "mayn shviger?" Zogt zhe aléyn -- ver den zol geshvoln vern, az nit mayn shviger?*
("Have you heard the explanation of *tizal katal imrosi*? So I'll tell you: *tizal -- should swell up; katal -- like a mountain; imrosi -- my mother-in-law.* You might ask, why is *tizal* 'should swell up?' But what should my mother-in-law do, if not swell up? So you'll ask again, why should *katal* mean '*like a mountain?*' If she's going to swell up, what should she swell up like? Like a pear? Of course like a mountain! What's that? You ask why is *imrosi* '*my mother-in-law?*' But *you* tell me -- who should swell up, if not my mother-in-law?" RP, p. 18.)

The humor here is simultaneously earthy and intellectual. In the first place, the whole joke is a parody of the process of glossing Hebrew texts by giving a Yiddish equivalent for each successive word: a process which every Jewish man knew intimately from his boyhood years in *kheyder* (traditional religious school). The Yiddish glosses of the root-morphemes of the Hebrew words are completely wrong, but the affixes are rendered correctly, so that there is a certain delicious plausibility about the translation. Thus *tizal* 'shall distil' is a feminine third person future imperfective verb, in a form which is often correctly translatable by a Yiddish *zol* 'should' plus verb: 'should swell up' or 'should distil' -- what's the difference! *Katal* 'like the dew' consists of the prefix *ka-* 'like' plus the root *tal* 'dew' -- so '*like* a mountain' isn't a bad translation. And *imrosi* 'my speech' is a feminine noun in the first person singular possessive form (*-i* 'my'), just like '*my* mother-in-law.'[184] Close enough! The

joke then proceeds with relentless logic. Once the hearer accepts
the gloss for any one of the three words, the others fall into place
according to the well known logical principle that anything follows
from a false premise.[185] In jokes like this the Yiddish curse has
been apotheosized into an art-form -- the snarl of hostility has been
sublimated into a laugh.

10.0   SWEARING OATHS

Among the most interesting of all psycho-ostensive expressions
are those related to the swearing of oaths. The purpose of an oath
is to convince the listener of the truth of a certain proposition.
This proposition may be phrased either positively or negatively:
either I swear to you that X is the case, or I swear to you that X is
not the case. Yiddish oaths all share a certain syntactic format.
They consist of two clauses standing in the same 'comparative' relationship to each other that we have just analyzed in connection with
elaborate, attenuated curses. One of these clauses contains the
optative auxiliary *zoln* 'may, would that' and usually the adverb *azóy*
'so'.[186] This part of the oath we may call the *juridical appeal*, or
the 'appeal,' for short. This is what the speaker 'swears by.' It
is in this clause that the speaker offers up to the listener something
which he hopes will be taken as irrefutable evidence bearing on the
truth-value of the proposition expressed in the other clause (which
is almost always introduced by the comparative conjunction *vi* 'as'):

$$zol \ldots azóy \ldots, \; vi + Clause.$$
$$\text{APPEAL} \qquad \text{PROPOSITION}$$

The appeal may purport to reflect any of three psychosemantic states.
In the simplest case, the speaker is swearing by something good which
he desires. This is the *auto-bono-petitive* appeal. More subtle and
complicated are appeals where the speaker seems to wish himself evil
(*auto-malo-petitive* appeals) and where he explicitly shuns evil for

himself (*auto-malo-fugitive* appeals). Each psychosemantic orienta-
tion of the appeal determines different inferences which the hearer
is invited to make as to the truth or falsity of the proposition
expressed in the other clause. Further, whether or not the proposition
may be negatively phrased depends on the particular type of appeal
used.

10.1 *Bono-Petitive Oaths*[187]

These are the simplest and most transparent of Yiddish oaths.
The speaker is saying, 'The proposition is true, as I wish good for
myself. You, the hearer, can put yourself in my place: you truly wish
good for yourself, so you must know that I also truly wish good for
myself. Thus you should be persuaded when I tell you that I am making
my sought-for good *contingent on* the truth of the proposition.' Behind this, of course, lies the shared belief of speaker and hearer
that if the proposition is false despite the oath to the contrary,
the speaker is somehow putting his own happiness in jeopardy.[188]

This is the only kind of oath in which the proposition may be
negatively phrased (i.e. may contain the negative adverb *nit* in its
surface structure).

Bono-petitive oaths may be subdivided according to the particular
good thing specified in the appeal: life, health, or future happiness.
In the commonest of all appeals, the speaker swears by his life,
using the formula:

(292) *zol ikh azóy lebn* ～ *ikh zol azóy lebn*[189] ("I should live
so [long]!").[190]

For example:

(293) *Zol ikh azóy lebn, vi ikh hob aykh gefunen a meydl vi gold!*
("I should live so, I've got for you a girl like gold!", i.e. "I
offer my life as warrant that I have found you an exemplary young
lady.")

With a negated proposition:

(294) <u>*Ikh*</u> *zol azóy lebn, vi ikh hob aykh keyn mol nit ópgenart!*
("I should live so, I've never cheated you once!")

As an even stronger oath, the speaker may swear by the lives of his
family -- wife, children, affines -- as well as his own:

(295) *zol ikh mit mayn vayb un kinder azóy lebn*   ("may I and my
wife and children live so long!").

Oaths like this are to be reserved for highly serious occasions.
People look with contempt on those who take the lives of their fami-
lies so lightly that they are willing to 'risk' them to prove their
point in argument. Such behavior is sometimes referred to in Yiddish-
influenced American English as 'swearing up and down.' There is usually the feeling that the swearer is protesting too much, so that
paradoxically the stronger oath is less likely to be believed than
the weaker one.

The swearer sometimes has recourse to the trick of including his
hearer in the life-oath. This is a kind of trap. By saying:

(296) *zoln mir beyde azóy lebn* ("may we both live so long!"),

the speaker has injected the hearer's own hopes and fears into the
situation. The hearer (or so the swearer hopes) will be inclined to
accept the truth of the proposition, since his own life has, willy-
nilly, been staked on it:

(297) *Makht der ganef, "Zoln mir beyde azóy lebn, vi ikh bin nit
shuldik, un vi mir iz keyn mol nit áyngefaln tsu gánvenen."* ("Said
the thief, 'We should both live so long, I'm not guilty, and it has
never even entered my head to steal.' " RP, p. 96.)

Very similar are bono-petitive appeals to one's health, or that
of one's family, or of the hearer. The formula to use is *zol* <u>*ikh*</u> *azóy
zayn gezúnt* 'so may I be healthy,' or one of its variants:[191]

(298) *A modne zakh! Zol ikh azóy gezúnt zayn, un zoln mir ale azóy
gezúnt zayn un úndzere gute fraynt oykh, vi mir hot zikh gekholemt*

der zélbiker kholem! ("A strange thing! So may I be healthy, and so may we all be healthy, and our good friends too, I dreamt the exact same dream!" RP, p. 28.)[192]

Finally, the swearer may pick any desirable event that he longs to see come to pass, and appeal to it in his oath. A key word here is *derlebn* 'live to experience something':

(299) *zoln mir azóy derlebn al dos guts*   ("so may we live to see all good things");

(300) *zol ikh mit mayn vayb azóy hobn a gutn elter* ("so may my wife and I have a good old age");

(301) *zoln mir azóy derlebn tsu zen nakhes fun úndzere kinder un kinds kinder* ("so may we live to see *nakhes* from our children and children's children");[193]

(302) *zol ikh azóy derlebn khásene tsu makhn mayne kinder* ("so may I live to marry off my children");

(303) *zol ikh azóy derlebn tsu firn Nadja'n tsu der khupe* ("so may I live to lead Nadja to the wedding-canopy"), etc.

10.2 *Auto-Malo-Petitive Oaths*

We have seen that it is possible to swear that something is not the case via a bono-petitive oath with overtly negated proposition [*above (294), (297)*]. The same semantic effect may be achieved more indirectly by using an oath whose appeal is auto-malo-petitive but whose proposition is *not* overtly negated. To say 'As I wish for evil to come to me, so X is the case' is to invite the hearer to reason as follows: 'He does not really wish for evil to come to him; therefore X cannot be true.' The usual expression one uses in such an appeal is *zol ikh azóy visn fun beyz* 'so may I know of evil':[194]

(304) *Zol ikh azóy visn fun beyz, vi ikh veys, vos ba mir tut zikh!* ("So may I know of evil, the way I know about what's going on in my house!" i.e., "I swear to you that I don't know what's going on in

my house." RP, p.61.)

(305) *Zol ikh azóy visn fun beyz, vi ikh farshtéy epes in maslines.*
("So may I know of evil, the way I understand anything about
olives." i.e., "I swear to you that I know nothing whatever about
olives." RP, p. 164.)

More picturesque versions of this appeal are possible:

(306) *Zol ikh azóy visn fun tsaar[195] un fun tsores un fun grine
verem, vi ikh farshtéy a vort, vos der blat shraybt do.* ("So may I
know of misery and trouble and green worms, the way I understand a
word of what's written here in the newspaper!" *L'Chayim*, p. 115.)

As the examples show, the verb of the proposition is usually a
verb of knowing, just as the verb of appeal is, making for a neat
parallelism between the clauses. These malo-petitive oaths are thus
a favorite way of making *protestations of ignorance*. One is reminded
of the English expression, *Damned if I know!*[196,197]

10.3 *Malo-Fugitive Oaths*

One further type of Yiddish oath is possible, even though it is
very peculiar from the point of view of logic. One may negate the
malo-petitive appeal-formula of the previous section, so that it
becomes malo-fugitive:

(307) *zol ikh (azóy) nit visn fun beyz/keyn shlekhts* ("so may I
not know from any evil").

As in the malo-petitive case, the following proposition is never
overtly negative. One might therefore expect *a priori* that the
Yiddish hearer would interpret such an oath in the opposite way from
that of the previous section, i.e. as a protestation that the positive
proposition *is in fact true*. One would think that a sentence like,

(308) *Zol ikh nit visn fun beyz, vi ikh veys, fun vos di gvirim
hobn azá hanoe!* ("So may I not know from evil, the way I know
what rich men take such pleasure in!" RP, p. 48.),

would be interpreted as follows: 'It is true that the swearer does not want to know of evil, as he claims in his appeal; therefore he *does* in fact know what rich men take such pleasure in.' By this interpretation, the malo-fugitive appeal has the same effect as a bono-petitive one would:

(308a) *Zol ikh azóy lebn, vi ikh veys X!* ("I should live so, I know X!")

But this is in fact an impossible interpretation. For the Yiddish hearer the malo-fugitive appeal determines exactly the same truth-value for the proposition as the malo-petitive one does. Sentence (308) can only mean that the swearer is claiming *not* to know what rich men take pleasure in. There is no simple relationship between logic and natural language![198]

10.4 *Manipulation Of Oaths For Special Effects*

Yiddish oaths, like their counterparts in other languages, are not always to be taken at face value. First there is the obvious fact that any juridical appeal may be used cynically by a swearer who wishes to deceive his hearer. But even leaving that aside, the appeals may be deliberately played with, parodied, or confused for humorous or literary effect.

For one thing, one may playfully convert an *auto*-malo-petitive appeal into an *allo*-malo-petitive one. Suppose you are discussing the incompetence of a certain doctor, and swearing that you will never entrust yourself to his care. This may be done in a relatively straightforward way by using an auto-malo-petitive appeal that is phrased in such a way that it has medical relevance:

(309) *Zol ikh azóy hobn a shnit in boykh, vi ikh ken zikh farlozn oyf dem dokter!* ("So may I have my belly cut, the way I can trust that doctor!")

That is, I can trust him as much as I would like to see my belly ripped open -- not at all. Yet if you are feeling humorously malicious you may sneak into the appeal words like *bay im* 'on him,' thus:

(310) *Zol ikh azóy hobn bay im a shnit in boykh, vi ...* ("So may
I have my belly cut on him...").

From one point of view this sentence is now nonsensical, but it does
succeed in doing two things at once: cursing the doctor and swearing
an oath of non-trust. An analogous English gambit would be to say
something like 'Cross my heart and hope you die, if I'm telling you
a lie.'

We may close with the brilliant *bon mot* that expresses the truism
that everybody wants to go on living:

(311) *Zol <u>ikh</u> azóy lebn, vi ikh vil shtarbn.* ("I swear by my life
that I want to die." RP, p. 179.)

The appeal is bono-petitive in form, and the proposition is not negated, so that the oath would normally be interpreted as inviting the
hearer to believe the proposition's truth -- i.e., that I really want
to die. Yet the content of the proposition is such that it contra-
dicts the literal meaning of the appeal, giving rise to the sort of
piquant paradox that Jewish humor delights in: the oath only has force
if one believes in the sincerity of the appeal, yet if the appeal is
taken as sincere then the proposition must be true, but if the proposition is true then the appeal is insincere, and so on round and
round.[199]

11.0   CONCLUSION AND COMMENCEMENT

The time has come to try to weave together the various themes
that have run like so many unruly threads through the homespun fabric
of this book.

11.1 *Syntactic Properties Of Psycho-Ostensive Expressions*

We have not attempted any 'rigorous' analysis of the syntactic

properties of these expressions. This is not an uninteresting topic--
but it has not seemed worthwhile to get sidetracked from our main concerns, which are psychosemantic in nature.

Among the questions that lend themselves to further syntactic
investigation, we may mention the following:

(a) *Independent vs. parenthetical use.* We have seen that most
psycho-ostensive formulas can serve as independent utterances all by
themselves, when the context is sufficiently clear from the discourse
or the extra-linguistic situation:[200]

(189) *Nu, vos makht epes ayer zun?* ("So how's your son?")
　　　 Keyn ayn-hore! ("No evil-eye!")

In fact, it seems plausible to 'derive' even parenthetically used
formulas from independent sentences. Witness the fact that even
questions may function as parenthetical psycho-ostensives:

(270) *Mayn vayb -- darf zi lebn? -- hot dos im avékgegebn umzíst.*
("My wife -- must she live? -- gave it away to him for nothing.")

Yet the relationship between independent and parenthetical usage
is not a simple one. Some psycho-ostensives never make it to the
surface as complete utterances by themselves (e.g., mortuo-bono-
petitives like *olevasholem,* above 8.0a). Others resist parenthesiza-
tion, usually because of their excessive length. It is unusual to
find sentences like:

(312) *Zayn eydem -- zol er vaksn vi a tsíbele, mitn kop in drerd
-- hot dos mir farkóyft.* ("His son-in-law -- may he grow like an
onion with his head in the earth -- sold it to me.")

To try to formalize observations like these -- how long must a formula
be before it becomes unnatural or impossible to encapsulate it into a
larger sentence -- is a thankless -- and I say this without any fear
of contradiction -- task.[201]

(b) *Constituency.* Once a formula is incorporated parenthetically
into a larger sentence, the question arises as to what it is in constituency with on the surface. Sometimes a formula is clearly

attributive to some noun of the larger sentence, in the manner of an adjective or relative clause:

(97) *Hot fun der geshikhte gehért der rov, zol gezúnt zayn.* ("So the rabbi, may he be healthy, heard about the whole business.")

In many other cases, the formula seems to function rather like a sentence adverbial, modifying the verb of the larger sentence, or what amounts to the same thing, the larger sentence as a whole:

(178) *Dem kúmendikn zumer vel ikh, im yirtse hashém, farbrengn afn breg-yam.* ("I'll spend next summer at the seashore, if God wills it.")

Each particular formula seems unique in the degree of looseness or tightness with which it is bound to the larger sentence, or to a subpart thereof.

(c) *Permutability.* With parenthesized formulas there is the further question as to the particular point in the larger sentence where the insertion may take place. Very often more than one ordering is possible. Consider where the formula *oyf ale yidn gezógt gevorn* 'may it be said of all Jews' may be inserted into the following sentence:

(313) *'S iz dortn gevén tsúgegreyt a sude kiyad-hameylekh.* ("There was there prepared a sumptuous banquet.")

At least three variants are possible:

(313a) *Oyf ale yidn gezógt gevorn, 's iz dortn gevén tsúgegreyt a sude kiyad-hameylekh.*

(313b) *'S iz dortn gevén tsúgegreyt, oyf ale yidn gezógt gevorn, a sude kiyad-hameylekh.*

(313c) *'S iz dortn gevén tsúgegreyt a sude kiyad-hameylekh, oyf ale yidn gezógt gevorn.*

While it is easy to give labels to each of these insertion-patterns -- we could call them *anticipatory, intercalated,* and *resumptive,* respectively -- it is less easy to determine what differences of meaning or emphasis are associated with each alternative ordering. Even harder would be to formulate rules that would predict when alternative orderings would be possible in the first place.

Such are the walls against which I have chosen not to bang my head. The real interest of psycho-ostensive expressions lies elsewhere.

11.2 *The Atomic Psychic States And Their Interrelationships*

We have been talking primarily about the inner psychic states which underlie the use of the formulas. How well have we isolated the individual psychosemantic components of such familiar speech acts as thanks, blessings, curses, oaths, and the rest? How well have we translated the elusive inner language of our mental processes into the pseudo-precise language of expository prose? *Traduttori traditori*, no matter what. And yet to me these categories inspire a degree of confidence precisely because they are imprecise. Concepts like *recognitive/fugitive/petitive* are not considered as mutually exclusive compartmentalizations of psychosemantic space, but rather as different aspects of the same thing: the human organism's often confused and ambiguous response to the outside world. We have constantly emphasized how intimately the various psychic states are related to each other, how easily they shade into each other: to seek future good is to flee future evil [auto-bono-petitive/auto-malo-fugitive, *3.0/7.0*]; we may fear future evil most when we are giving thanks for our present good fortune [auto-bono-recognitive/auto-malo-fugitive, *3.0*]; to wish others well may be a way of recognizing that one has himself received a good [allo-bono-petitive/auto-bono-recognitive, *3.0*]; to congratulate someone is simultaneously to recognize his present good and hope for his future good [allo-bono-recognitive/allo-bono-petitive, *3.0*]; by empathy we may feel another's experience of evil as keenly as our own [allo-malo-recognitive/auto-malo-recognitive, *4.0*]; we may compliment most sincerely when we are appearing to criticize [allo-malo-recognitive/allo-bono-recognitive, 7.5], etc.[202]

   This raises the question of whether it would be profitable to transfer the deep/surface dichotomy into the psychosemantic realm, and to distinguish between 'underlying' vs. 'superficial' psychic states. This is clearly an area where linguists must be guided by their psychologist brethren, who have been operating with notions like 'conscious' vs. 'subconscious' feelings for generations. Surely the time is ripe for linguists to involve themselves more deeply in these questions. Perhaps, for example, we could say that the Yiddish speaker, even when he is not being purposefully mendacious, uses psycho-ostensive expressions on two levels. At a moment in the dis- course when the Yiddish language and Jewish culture require him to use such a formula -- e.g. when mentioning an achievement of his child, or pronouncing the name of a dead close relative -- he says what is expected of him (*may he live 120 years* or *may he rest in peace* or whatever). In many cases his subconscious feelings are not in con- flict with his verbalization of them, so that the 'deep' and 'super- ficial' psycho-semantic structures coincide. Sometimes, however, such a conflict does exist -- the *mixed feelings* situation. Perhaps his pride in his child's achievement is mixed up with defensive feel- ings of jealousy, which the pronouncing of the formula helps to re- press. The psycho-ostensives can thus have a 'filtering' function, allowing only the socially acceptable feelings to rise to conscious- ness.

11.3 *Involvement vs. Detachment: Compulsion vs. Freedom In The Use Of Psycho-Ostensives*

   Any use of language is a compromise between freedom and bondage. The speaker usually has a free choice of *what* he is going to say, though the conventions of his language dictate *how* he must say it if he wishes to be understood by others. Sometimes the linguistic or extra-linguistic context is such that the speaker's freedom of choice is minimal. When you answer the phone, you'd better say *Hello.*

Yiddish psycho-ostensives generally lie on this compulsory side of the spectrum.[203] When you mention a dreaded event, you had better use a malo-fugitive formula. If you don't, your interlocutor will give you a disapproving glance and interject one for you.

Nevertheless, the Yiddish speaker retains considerable freedom to manipulate the psycho-ostensive formulas for his own purposes. These ulterior motives may be either benign or hypocritical. In the benign case, the speaker plays with the formulas to show off his virtuosity, or to make his listener laugh. We have seen numerous examples of jokes whose humor revolves entirely around the inappro- priate or paradoxical use of psycho-ostensives: the thief's use of malo-recognitive *nebekh* to lament his deserved punishment (38); the gradual shift from bono-petitive to malo-petitive formulas as the marriage-broker talks about his wife (101); the sarcastic use of the malo-fugitive *kholile* to attack hypocrisy (144-145); the mortuo-bono- petitive formulas for the former patients of the 'wonderful' doctor (208); the quibbling about using a polite pronoun in a curse (note 166); oaths which are manipulated for special effects (section 10.4). The fact that these 'misuses' of the formulas are so funny is ample proof that all competent Yiddish speakers are thoroughly aware of their normal functions.

More hypocritically, the psycho-ostensive formulas may be used with a conscious intent to deceive one's listener, as a mask for one's true feelings. We may use a mortuo-bono-petitive formula in honor of someone whom we still hate bitterly (Intro.); utter insincere auto-malo-recognitive formulas in pseudo-sympathy, like the woman who wrung her hands after making sure her egg-basket was safe (26); swear oaths by all that is holy, even though the proposition sworn to is entirely false (297-298), etc. These cases are subtly different from the 'mixed feelings' situation described above, where the speaker may not be aware of the difference between what he is saying and what he is 'feeling deep down.'

Also worthy of mention in the context of freedom vs. compulsion is the *euphemistic* use of psycho-ostensives. Here the difference

between what is overtly said and what is covertly felt is not intended
to deceive. Neither is is intended to make the listener laugh. In
these cases the speaker feels *compelled* by the social conventions or
ethical values of the culture to say the opposite of what he means.[204]

11.4   *The Expressive Function Of Language: Word-Power*

Yiddish psycho-ostensives may be evaluated from still another
point of view. Especially in the case of curses, the formulas may
serve a purely therapeutic function. They are convenient, conventionalized ways of letting off steam -- releasing bursts of psychic energy
which might otherwise remain hopelessly bottled up, to the detriment
of the speaker's mental health. There is a story about a teamster who
had a particularly foul mouth (i.e. was much given to malo-petitive
expressions). One day a client offered him three extra rubles if he
could cover a certain distance without uttering a single curse. The poor
teamster controls himself as various mishaps occur to his wagon along
the route. Finally he gives up:

(314) *Shpringt er aróp fun vogn un loyft tsu tsum rod un shrayt:*
"A gezunte kholerye dir in boykh! Oy! Zeks rubl iz gelt, ober di
gezúnt iz táyerer!" ("So he jumps down from the wagon and runs over
to the wheel and shouts, 'A goddam cholera in your belly! Ah! Six
rubles is money, but my health comes first!' " RP, p. 162.)

One final story and I have done. Several Jews are playing cards, when
all of a sudden one of them drops dead in an apoplectic fit. How are
the others to break the news gently to his wife? Finally one of them
sees a way. He goes to the widow's house and says:

(315) *"Ir veyst, Khaye-Beyle, ayer man hot geshpilt in kortn un hot*
óngevorn finf hundert karbn." Heybt di yídene on tsu geváldeven:
"A kholerye oyf im! Péygern zol er, der hunt, der kelev, der
sobake!" Makht der yid: "Fun ayer moyl in Gots oyern, er iz take
geshtorbn!" (" 'You know, Khaye-Beyle, your husband was playing
cards and lost 500 rubles.' At this the woman began shrieking,

'A cholera on him! May he croak, the dog, the cur, the mongrel!'
Said the man, 'From your mouth to God's ears! He did die, in fact.'"
RP, p. 40.)205

This would not be funny if everybody didn't realize that curses are
not usually meant to be taken literally, but are rather quasi-
therapeutic outbursts of psychic energy.

Jewish proverbial wisdom constantly emphasizes the awesome power
of speech, the dangers of enshrining temporary psychic states in a
hostile verbal form which may be permanently remembered:

(316) *A beyze tsung iz erger fun a shlekhter hant.* ("A wicked
tongue is worse than an evil hand." YP, p. 12.)

(317) *Di gantse velt shteyt oyf der shpits tsung.* ("The whole
world stands on the tip of the tongue." YP, p. 60.)

(318) *A patsh fargéyt, a vort bashtéyt.* ("A blow subsides, a word
abides." YP, p. 22.)

(319) *A vort iz azóy vi a fayl -- beyde hobn groyse ayl.* ("A word
is like an arrow -- they both go a long way." YP, p. 26.)

Among many other such proverbs,206 the following two seem especially
significant:

(320) *Eyzehu giber? Ha-koyvesh a glaykh-vertl.* ("Who is to be
called mighty? He who suppresseth a wisecrack." YP, p. 70.)207

(321) *Fun yídishe reyd ken men zikh nit ópvashn in tsen vasern.*
("Ten waters will not cleanse you of Jewish talk." YP, p. 76.)

In traditional Jewish society, verbal brilliance often functioned
as a compensatory substitute for action in the real world. If one
could not in actual fact kill the czar or beat up a truculent Polish
peasant, at least one could sublimate one's hostility and fear by
eloquent and cynical humor. Yet nobody was really fooled by this:

(322) *Nit mit shiltn un nit mit lakhn, ken men di velt íbermakhn.*
("Neither with cursing nor with laughter can one remake the world."
YP, p. 96.)208

12.0 *EPES AN ÉPILOG:* THE RELEVANCE OF YIDDISH PSYCHO-OSTENSIVES TO
RECENT AND FUTURE WORK IN LINGUISTICS AND OTHER FIELDS[209]

(a) *Field linguistics, anthropology, ethnography, folklore*

All languages have some kind of verb-like word-class which is
distinguishable from a noun-like class of entities -- but there are
enormous differences of detail in the morphological, syntactic, and
semantic properties of the 'nouns' vs. the 'verbs' from one linguistic
area of the world to the other.[210] A universalist approach emphasizes
the deep structural similarities among all human languages despite
their surface diversity. A relativistic approach prefers to stress
this very diversity, insisting that the categories useful in describing one language are not necessarily applicable mechanically to a
language of a very different genetic or typological nature. Despite
the recent imbalance in linguistics in favor of universalistic
theorizing [*see section 1.0*], it is now becoming clear to everybody
that both types of linguistic investigation have their rightful place
in the world. A good linguist should be able to change his viewpoint
according to his purposes of the moment, appreciating both the ways in
which languages are similar and the ways in which they differ. A
visual analogy is the cube ⬡ , where one or another facet may be
given prominence by the   perceiver at any moment:[211]

The study of psycho-ostensive formulas may also be undertaken from
both the 'universalizing' and 'particularizing' points of view. It is
exciting to discover cross-linguistic similarities between the formulas of Yiddish and, say, Greek and Turkish. But after the initial
excitement has subsided, come the questions. Are the expressions
alike because one language borrowed them from the other? Historical
linguists can trace innumerable cases of such *loan translations* or
calques among languages in close cultural contact.[212] Or, on the other

hand, perhaps the expressions are similar *by accident* -- or, what sometimes seems to amount to the same thing -- because of universal ten-
dencies of human language and psychology.[213]

The Turkish/Greek/Yiddish case is especially interesting. Nobody
can deny that Turkey and Greece belong to the same culture area, that
wonderful part of the world called the Levant, crossroads of civiliza-
tions, where people from out of Durrell's novels -- whether in Alexan-
dria, Beirut, Athens, Yerevan, Nicosia, or Izmir -- go around having
the same figs and yoghurt for breakfast, and halvah or baklava for
dessert. Greeks (Herodotus, for one) have lived in Asia Minor since
antiquity, and the two peoples have been in intimate cultural contact
ever since the Turks' arrival in the Near East from their ancestral
Altaic homeland in Central Asia.

But Jews have also been an integral part of the Levantine scene
for millennia. In the broader perspective the Levant is only part of
the whole Mediterranean World, comprising Arabic North Africa (the
Maghreb), the Iberian Peninsula, Southern France, and Italy as well,
a vast region which has had a certain cultural unity ever since the
days of the Roman Empire. The Jews continuing to live around the
Mediterranean littoral have traditionally been called *Sephardic*, in
contrast to the *Ashkenazic* branch of the Jewish people, whose wander-
ings took them up the Rhine Valley, into Germany, and eventually all
over Eastern Europe.[214] The Yiddish language was developed in the
Ashkenazic branch. Sephardic Jews spoke all the tongues of the
Mediterranean, but the most distinctively Jewish language they used
was an outgrowth of medieval Spanish variously known as Ladino, Judeo-
Spanish, or Judezmo.

My colleague Martin Schwartz, a distinguished amateur ethno-
musicologist,[215] has collected overwhelming evidence to show that the
lively Jewish *klezmer* music which is familiar to any American Jew who
has ever been to a fancy wedding or Bar Mitzvah is in fact practically
indistinguishable from certain varieties of popular Greek, Turkish,
and Armenian music. This presents an intriguing paradox. The Jews
of Greece and Turkey are Sephardic,[216,217] but those now in the U.S.

are almost all Ashkenazim. Yet Sephardic Jewish music sounds, if anything, less like Greek/Turkish music than Ashkenazic music does!
Whatever the explanation may prove to be,[218] it is easy to imagine
that the elaborate use of psycho-ostensive expressions might also have
been a diffused trait throughout the vast Mediterranean and Eastern
European cultural areas.[219]

A language's psycho-ostensive formulas do, in fact, furnish
excellent clues to its cultural preoccupations. In rural Greece, one
takes leave of a pregnant woman with *me to ghio* 'with the son.'[220]
It is easy to deduce that male issue are highly valued in the culture.

As the ongoing researches of maledictionists are making clear
[*see note 155*], there are similarities in the nature of verbal abuse
the world over, though the nuances and emphases are different according to culture area and historical period. The three realms of *sex,
scatology,* and *blasphemy* just about exhaust the possibilities for
human cursing, but the proportions in the mixture are very different
between, say, medieval France and the modern Soviet Union.

The Japanese, like the British, are trained from childhood to
control or suppress linguistic and paralinguistic cues to their actual psychic states. It is good manners in Japan to smile when telling
somebody else about a death in one's own family, or indeed when con-
veying bad news of any kind. In Jewish culture the only way to make
sense of such behavior would be to assume that the bereaved but smiling
person had gone temporarily mad from grief. (The 'normal' person
would be weeping, and uttering auto-malo-recognitive laments, vivo-
bono-petitives, mortuo-bono-petitives, auto- and allo-malo-fugitives,
and generally giving as much linguistic expression to his complex and
turbulent emotions as he could.)[221]

The differences and the similarities in psycho-ostensive behavior
across cultures are equally instructive, and a concerted attack on the
problem by linguists, anthropologists, cultural historians, ethnopsychiatrists, and folklorists would be of mutual benefit to all these
fields.

(b) *Sociolinguistics*

Perhaps as an antidote to the overemphasis in early generative grammar on productive, rule-governed syntactic processes, there is now a countersurge of interest on the part of semantic theorists in those vast areas of language that are 'prefabricated' and learned by rote: collocations, ready-made formulas, *expressions toutes faites,* idioms, clichés, aphorisms.[222]

The interactional nature of many of these formulas had been clearly perceived already by Zimmer (1958), who connected them implicitly with the Zipfian principle of *least expenditure of effort* in human affairs:

"Situational formulas serve as the linguistic reaction to definable situations without imposing a burden of formulation on the speaker."[223]

The security of knowing *the right thing to say* in a given situation is a precious commodity. The loss of such security is keenly felt by speakers who have to switch from speaking a language rich in psycho-ostensives to one that is relatively poor in them. As Zimmer says (p. 14):

"I have myself observed that native speakers of German who have lived in Turkey for some time would frequently use Turkish situational formulas such as *estağfurullah* in a German context."

Tannen reports that after a sojourn in Greece, when her American friends say *Welcome back* to her, she automatically replies *Well I found you.*[224] East European Jews who take up residence in Israel frequently confess that they feel funny because Hebrew has only a single stylistic level for second-person pronouns (*ata* [masc.], *at* [fem.]), while Yiddish has the familiar (*du*) vs. polite (*ir*) distinction. A similar nostalgia for Yiddish psycho-ostensives has motivated their extensive calquing in Israeli Hebrew [*see notes 58, 125*].

Psycho-ostensive expressions are, in fact, habit-forming. They are a wonderful social lubricant.

(c) *Psychosemantics, psychology, psychotherapy*

I suggest the term *psychosemantics* for the new branch of linguistics that concerns itself with the relationship between psychological states and their linguistic or paralinguistic expression.[225]
This relationship is marvelously complex, since we transmit and receive
our communicative signals on many different channels simultaneously.
Often body language and tone of voice are more revealing of the speaker's underlying psychic state than the actual words uttered [*see section 1.0, above*].

We often don't know ourselves what our true feelings are in a
given situation. Our personalities are labyrinthine constructs, with
layers of defense mechanisms and projections that distort our per-
ceptions of ourselves and others. Although some cultures do seem to
place a special premium on not showing directly by word or deed what
one is feeling, children in *all* cultures quickly learn not to say the
first thing that pops into their heads, lest they give offense to
others or reveal a weakness of their own. There seem to be good, sound
evolutionary reasons for this. Animal behaviorists[226] tell us that
it is often quite hard to tell that a bird is sick until it is practically dead. This is because the bird puts on specious health dis-
plays with every ounce of its waning strength -- if it were to admit
its illness by droopy behavior, the other birds would quickly peck it
to death. Deviousness has a certain survival value, for man or beast.

We may confidently expect that as the field of psychosemantics
develops, it will put forth more specialized offshoots of its own.
The linguistic powers and potentialities of the mind are still so
imperfectly known.[227] On the far horizon one can even see --
hypnolinguistics! Hypnosis has been around a long time, but the recent
resurgence of interest in the field is largely due to the surpassing
brilliance of the work of the hypnotherapist, Milton H. Erickson,
M.D.[228] The analysis of transcripts of Erickson's hypnotic patter
reveals extremely subtle verbal manipulation of the states of consciousness of the subject.[229] Irony, euphemism, sarcasm, innuendo

-- every rhetorical wrinkle we have seen in operation in our psycho-
ostensive expressions -- is put at the service of the therapeutic task
as the hypnotist strives to communicate with the patient's unconscious
mind, which works not by rational logic but by *metaphor*. There is no
question of 'hypocrisy' or 'deception.' The therapeutic situation is
amoral. The doctor is doing it for the patient's own good.

The *transactional analysis* popularized by Eric Berne, M.D.[230]
could well have ramifications within the field of psychosemantics.
Berne gives catchy, easy-to-remember names to the interactional linguistic 'games that people play' so that his patients will recognize
them for what they are. When you name something, you gain power over
it. If your spouse can say to you "Your 'child' just hooked my
'parent,' and we're playing *I'm-being-naughty-to-see-if-you-really-
love-me-enough-to-punish-me*" -- then you know the jig is up, and you've
got to find some other game to play. The careful observer can learn
to associate certain linguistic and paralinguistic features with certain subparts of his own and others' personalities -- in transactional
terms, the *child, adult,* and *parent* that coexist within all human
psyches.[231]

Under great emotional stress, or when one lets his guard down for
a moment, speech patterns associated with one's early childhood can
reassert themselves, despite having been suppressed for decades
since.[232] My wife's mother's native language was Swedish, though she
has not used it at all since early childhood. On a trip to Sweden in
her forties she was suddenly thrown into a situation where she absolutely had to speak Swedish to her long lost relatives. Struggling
for a while as she age-regressed in her own inner Time Machine,
suddenly something clicked and she began speaking more and more
fluent Swedish -- *but at the top of her lungs*. No one could figure
out why she was shouting so loud, until somebody remembered that *her*
mother had been deaf.

This book has touched upon many issues in linguistics in what I
hope has been a *seykhl-farbréyterndik* kind of way.[233] If it has

provided few answers, at least it has been faithful to the Jewish tradition of answering a question with another question. What is an
'answer' anyway? As it is written,

(323) *Oyf itlekhn terets ken men gefinen a naye kashe.* ("For each
answer one can find a new question." YP, p. 100.)

NOTES

1. See, e.g., Chomsky 1957.

2. For a discussion of metaphorical associations between body-parts and the emotions in Tibeto-Burman, see Matisoff 1978a, pp. 210-213.

3. This sentence itself is a case in point.

4. All Yiddish words cited in this book are normalized into the standard language or *klal-shprakh* favored by the YIVO Institute for Jewish Research, now located in New York (formerly the *Yidisher Visnsháftlekher Institút* of Vilna). The transcription used was developed by Uriel Weinreich (1949, 1968). Note especially the use of *kh* to represent the voiceless velar fricative [χ].

   Hebrew-derived words occurring in a Yiddish context are transcribed as they are pronounced in Yiddish. In etymologies, however, the original Hebrew expressions are usually conventionally cited in their modern Israeli ('Sephardic') pronunciations. (Thus, e.g. *yasher-koyekh* < Heb. *yiyshar koakh* [see below, sentence (9)].).

   Stress in Yiddish is overwhelmingly on the penultimate syllable. (Syllabic nasals and *-l* count as full syllables). When the stress falls elsewhere, we indicate it in our transcription, even though this is not the practice in ordinary Yiddish orthography: *gezúnt, késhene, mílkhikn*. See Weinreich 1968, pp. xxii - xxiii.

5. Or should I have said 'expanded and contracted?' What's the difference? Which sounds better? Which is more grammatical?

6. Linguists like to make fun of philosophers who speak of 'abuses of language.' But many generative linguists also seem to have prescriptive ideas about what is grammatical and what is not.

7. Or should he have said 'have I told you?'

8. See for example Fillmore 1971.

9. Taken from an article in the *New York Times*, 1978.

10. The insertion of a comma between 'dangerous' and 'addictive' helps to disambiguate the sentence in favor of the latter interpretation.

In spoken language, of course, the two alternatives could be distinguished by intonation.

11. See Chafe 1970, 1973, 1974.

12. See for example Leo Rosten 1968. For a review of this book see Chana Bloch 1969, 'Peddling Yiddish.'

13. I remember once composing an exercise to illustrate the Yiddish dative case for a language laboratory tape. My sentence *Gib dem kind a knish* ("Give the child a *knish*") was edited out by my co-workers in favor of the more 'cultural' sentence *Gib dem kind a mikroskóp* ("Give the child a microscope").

14. Or, to use the more simple terminology we shall introduce later, 'is bono-petitively disposed' to his son.

15. Especially among older, European-born speakers, the only segment of the American Yiddish-speaking population among whom Yiddish survives in its full richness.

16. These are examples of benedictive expressions that are not parenthetical but used as independent sentences in their own right. *See below 11.1.*

17. The page references ["RP"] are to Immanuel Olsvanger's splendid collection of Yiddish jokes and stories, *Röyte Pomerantsen* ("Blood Oranges"), 1965, from which we have taken many of our examples. Most of the stories in this book and Olsvanger's subsequent collection, *L'Chayim* ("To Life!"), were originally published in Europe in two volumes: *Rosinkes mit Mandlen* ("Raisins and Almonds"), 1921, and *Reyte Pomeranzen*, 1935. See the Foreword and the Bibliography.

18. The 'gratitude attitude' we could call it.

19. It is said that cats sometimes purr for this very reason, e.g. while being mauled by a child that it does not dare attack.

20. See the discussion of *malo-fugition*, section 7 below.

21. Hanan J. Ayalti (1963) translates it as "A Jew's joy is not without fright" (p.55). Henceforth we cite this work as "YP."

22.   See below 11.1 *et passim*.   In Turkish also, one often answers
the question "How are you?" with *Hamdelsun* ("Thank God").   (See Tannen
and Öztek, Turkish Appendix, No. 119).

23.   *Dir* is the familiar second person singular dative pronoun; *aykh*
is the plural or polite-singular counterpart.   If you insist, we may
make a terminological distinction between *theo-bono-recognition*
(thanking God) and *anthropo-bono-recognition* (thanking one's fellow
man).

24.   *A sheynem dank*, lit. 'a pretty thanks,' is directly comparable
to German *danke schön* (lit. 'thanks prettily').   Note that in English
we cannot thank prettily, though we can say *pretty please* (with or
without sugar on top).

25.   Often *Vos makht ir?* ("How are you?") is answered by ironic formulas like *Vos zol ikh makhn?* ("How should I be?"), *Me lebt un me
matert zikh* ("We live and we suffer"), etc.

26.   The Japanese react somewhat similarly to compliments.   It is
gauche in the extreme (in fact it is almost uninterpretable behavior)
to say 'Thank you' to a compliment.   One must rather say *Doo
itashimashite* 'What could I have done [to provoke such a compliment]!'
Alternatively, one may deny the compliment by the simple word *Iie*
'No!'

27.   The same is often true when *replying* to someone else's thanks.
Where we would say *You're welcome* after having been thanked, e.g. for
some food, the Yiddish speaker would usually respond with a blessing
like *Zol dir zayn tsu gezúnt* ("May it be to your health").

Another common way to say *You're welcome* is also bono-petitive:
zol dir voyl bakumen ("may it be happily received to you").

One thing that *cannot* be done in Yiddish is to use the same ex-
pression for *you're welcome* as for *please* (cf. French *je vous en prie,*
Italian *prego,* German *bitte,* Russian *pozháluJsto,* etc.).   [*Please* in
Yiddish is usually *zay/zayt azóy gut,* lit. "be so good as to..."].

For the negative way of expressing *you're welcome,* see note 28.

28.   As in many other languages it is also possible in Yiddish to say
you're welcome by the *via negativa*, by denying that there is any
cause for thanks: *nitó far vos* ("There is nothing for which [to be
thanked]").   Cf. Eng. *don't mention it*, Spanish *de nada*, French
de rien or *il n'y a pas de quoi*, Russian *nichevó*, Japanese *iie*, etc.

29.   As Olsvanger puts it, 'To thank the benefactor directly would be
to diminish the merit of giving' (*ibid.*).

This book *L'Chayim* ("To Life!") is Olsvanger's sequel to RP.
The word *lekhaim* is the standard formula used before tossing down an
alcoholic beverage.   Pre-potational formulas like this would make an
interesting cross-linguistic study.   Often they are bono-petitive
(Yid. *lekhaim*, Russ. *za zdorove*,   Fr. *à votre santé*, Eng. *to your
health*, Greek *stin ygheia sas*, etc.); sometimes they are psychosemantically neutral, referring only to the act of drinking itself
(Chinese *kanpei*, Japanese *kampai* "drain the cup!"; Eng. *bottoms up*,
Scandinavian *skål* [cf. Danish *skaal* 'bowl, cup']); occasionally, by
a teasing inversion, they are superficially malo-petitive (Eng. *here's
mud in your eye*).   [Thanks to Susan Matisoff for this last observation.   (*Here's looking at you, kid!*)].

30.   The writer's surname bears an unfortunate phonological resem-
blance to this locution, which exposed him to a certain amount of
teasing in his youth.

Miriam Petruck points out that the written form of the word *mazal*
itself has auspicious meaning.   All the letters of the Hebrew alphabet
have a traditional numerical value (just as, e.g. V, X, L, in the
Roman alphabet have a value of 5, 10, and 50, respectively).   According to this reckoning, the three consonant-letters of *mazal* have a
combined value of 77 (*mem* = 40, *zayin* = 7, *lamed* = 30), a very lucky
number indeed.   (The search for hidden numerological meanings in the
interpretation of sacred texts was especially characteristic of the
cabalistic tradition of esoteric Jewish philosophy.)

31.   The Turkish congratulatory expression used specifically to someone who has a acquired a house is *güle güle oturun* 'stay laughingly'

(Tannen and Öztek [18]).   See below 6.2 for analogies between Turkish *güle güle* and the Yiddish bono-petitive *gezunterhéyt*.

Another Turkish bono-recognitive formula aimed at a specific happy event is *gözünüz aydın*, lit. 'your eye sparkling,' used to someone who is enjoying the visit of a loved one.

32.   These expressions often appear negated, in which case they become malo-fugitive:

   a klog tsu mayn velt nit!   ("[May] a lament not [be] to my world!");

   a klog tsu mir nit!   ("[May] a lament not [be] to me!").

33.   The implication is that some disaster has occurred or will soon occur that father still knows nothing about, *not* that the speaker is wishing that his father's joy may change to sorrow.

34.   If one wishes to declare explicitly that he has no psychic energy to spare at the moment on the sorrows of others, he can say:

   (26a)   *Ikh hob éygene tsores.* ("I have troubles of my own" / "I've got things of my own to worry about.")

35.   See Rosten, *op. cit.*, pp. 260-2.   This word, like *mazltov*, is passing into general Amercian English, but only in its substantival usage.   A 'nebbish' is a hapless, ineffectual fellow, the object of everyone's amused or contemptuous sympathy (Yid. *a nebekh, a nébekhl*). *Nebekh* is of Slavic origin, probably from Czech *neboky*.

36.   The translation is perhaps infelicitous.   *Geshvólener oremán* means literally 'a swollen poor man' (bloated, as it were, with poverty).

37.   In these latter cases we might say that an unfortunate underlying copula has, *nebekh*, been deleted.

38.   See my *Grammar of Lahu* (1973), pp.330-1.   Lahu is a Tibeto-Burman language of the Loloish group.

39.   As one might expect, only three of the four possible subtypes of petitive states are found with any frequency: auto-bono-, allo-

bono-, and allo-malo. The masochistic state of auto-malo-petition receives linguistic expression in Yiddish mostly when swearing oaths, and even there it is obviously *pro forma* [*below 10.2*].

40. It probably derives ultimately from Aramaic. Very similar in meaning and syntactic properties in the Spanish word *ojalá* (ult. < Arabic *'in ša('a)llāh* 'if God wills it;' cf. Turkish *inšallah*). In our English glosses, we usually translate *halevây* conventionally by 'I hope ...'

41. For further remarks on the interesting optative word *oméyn*, see below 6.4.

42. Occasionally the auxiliary verb *gevorn* is omitted from the construction. See sentence (55). The Lahu liturgical language has a similar optative expression that focuses on "what others may say": *qāw-cà-law-cà* '[be so prosperous that] others will speak of [our good fortune].'

43. The more straightforward expression **shlekht yor* 'bad year' is never used, probably because it is too direct and horrible to utter. See the similarly 'too dangerous' sentence (254a), *below*.

44. The Jewish tradition is only one of many the world over which attach great importance to New Year's Day, and the repeated yearly cycle of dormancy, birth, heyday, and decay. The analogy between the seasons of the year and man's passage through life is so irresistible that it is perhaps a universal of human psychosemantics. See Walker 1970b.

45. In this connection, we might cite a rather well-worn witticism that Yiddish-speaking males sometimes utter upon seeing a pretty girl:

(59a) *Azá yor oyf mir, vi ikh oyf ir*. ("Such a year on me, as I on her," i.e. "The year should be as pleasant for me as it would be pleasant for me to be on top of her.")

46. Exceptions are expressions where God's help is invoked, which may be auto-petitive [*see section 6.2*].

47. This verb is really more medio-passive than truly reflexive or reciprocal. 'Go around wishing' is perhaps closer to the real idea. *Vintshn* (or the more emphatic *ónvintshn*) may also be used in malo-petitives. See sentence 197b, in note 139.

48. The word *bentshn* entered Yiddish at an early date, when Romance-speaking Jews were settled in the Rhine valley.

49. Life is no fun if one must go around, as the proverbial ex-pression has it, *mit híltsernem kop un glézerne oygn* 'with wooden head and glassy eyes.'

50. One may also apply this term to the satisfaction that a teacher derives from the accomplishments of his students. Thus my colleague Yakov Malkiel recently confessed that he reads the examination papers of his less good students with more attention than those of his best students. To linger too long on the latter would be to "wallow in *nakhes*."

51. A child who is a good *nakhes*-provider may be referred to as a *nákhesl*, with the diminutive suffix -*l*. This word may of course be used sarcastically, as when one parent is complaining to the other about the bad behavior of their child:

  (63a) *Ze nor, vos dayn nákhesl hot do gemákht.* ("Just take a look at what your little *nakhes*-machine did there!")

Very similar is the word *takhshet* (dim. *tákhshetl*), glossed only as 'brat' in Weinreich 1968 (p.375), but whose original Hebrew meaning was 'jewel.' The semantic shift arose through irony (see note 92). Cf. Eng. expressions like 'that prize son of yours.'

52. A slightly different emphasis is conveyed by this variant:

  (64a) *Kleyne kinder, kleyne tsores -- groyse kinder, groyse tsores.* ("Little children, *little* troubles -- big children, *big* troubles.")

53. An interesting concept is *góyisher nakhes* 'Gentile *nakhes*,' which means something like 'an inexplicable pleasure that one derives from doing something weirdly or dangerously un-Jewish,' like skin-

diving or rock-climbing. Thus if somebody, God forbid, should break
his leg while skiing, his friends are likely to reproach him by
saying:

(64b) *Vos hostu zikh gedárft zukhn góyisher nakhes?* ("Why did you
have to go looking for Gentile satisfactions?")

54. So far we are considering these blessings insofar as they occur
as complete utterances by themselves. We discuss them in their
'parenthetical' or 'encapsulated' guise in section 6.3.

55. By analogical extension, one can also feel *nakhes* toward the
children of one's brain.

56. For simplicity's sake, we give the beneficiary in all these expressions as second person singular. They may all be applied equally
well to second person plural or to any third person (pronominalized
or not): *a lebn tsu im!* ("Life to him!"); *a lebn tsu Niksonen* ("Life
to Nixon!").

57. In this expression *lebn* is the infinitive of the verb 'to live,'
not the homophonous noun meaning 'life.' Less idiomatic, but still
possible, is the uninverted order:

(66a) *Zolstu lang lebn!*

The Hebrew-derived expression *arikhas-yomim* 'length of days, longevity' may also be used in longevity-blessings:

(66b) *Zol dir Got arikhas-yomim gebn!* ("May God grant you long
days [on earth]!")

58. The expression "Be well!," used by some American Jews at the end
of a conversation or letter, is a calque on this Yiddish psycho-
ostensive, as is the modern Israeli Hebrew *tihye bari*.

59. Dov Noy points out that almost all of the expressions in sections
6.1 (a) and (b) may be used to a sneezer, though *tsu gezúnt*, being the
simplest, is the most common.

60. One may also say:

(75a) *A lebn tsu dayn kop!* ("A life to your head!"),

but never *A lebn dir in kop*, which sounds somehow ominous, reminding one of curses like *A veytik dir in kop* ("A pain to your head!"). *See section 9.3.*

Greek and Turkish also sometimes specify a particular body-part for the blessing to reach. Thus when a person has said something very apt, or when he has just told your fortune from coffee-grounds, you would say to him in Turkish *ağzına sağlık* 'health to your mouth' (Yid. *a gezúnt dir in moyl*). [This expression was chosen as the title of Tannen and Öztek 1977.]

Similarly, if someone has just shown you something he has made, or performed a service for you (like cooking dinner) that required a certain manual dexterity, you would say in Greek *gheia sta cheria sou* 'health to your hands,' or in Turkish *ellerin dert görmesin* 'may your hands never know trouble.' (This last expression is actually allo-malo-fugitive).

61. *Éyverl* is the diminutive of the Heb. *eyver* 'limb, organ, member.' According to traditional reckoning, there are 248 parts to the body. It is therefore quite a job to *óyskushn yeder éyverl* ("kiss [usually a child] on all his body-parts"). Other medical traditions are similarly precise about the number of parts in the body. Thus in Tibetan medicine the body was deemed to have exactly 900 *c'u-rgyus* 'sinews, ligaments, and nerves.' See Matisoff 1978, p. 166. As noted above [1.0], one does not have as free a choice of body-part for blessings as for curses. *See section 9.3.*

62. To someone who is actually seriously sick one usually wishes a *refue shleyme* 'complete recovery' (< Heb.):

(77a) *Zol dir Got gebn a refue shleyme.* ("May God grant you a complete recovery.")

Similar 'get well quick' formulas seem to exist in all languages: German *gute Besserung*, Turkish *geçmiş olsun*, etc.

63. The adverb *nor* 'only' very often appears as a reinforcer of blessings. It also crops up in the English of American Jews under Yiddish influence. ("You should only live and be well!").

A common rhymed variant of (80) is the following:

(80a) *Got zol dir nor gebn gezúnt un lebn!* ("May God only grant you health and life!")

64. Note the subtle preservation of the rhyme in our translation. This is actually an example of a *palliative blessing* [see below 6.2].

65. If the past participle is used it implies a more remote possibility that God would really do the job.

66. *Reb* is a polite morpheme that precedes the first name of a man, rather like Spanish *don*. To translate it 'don,' however, would introduce jarring connotations.

67. *Gmiles-khesed*, here translated 'loan,' actually means 'a freely-offered gift.' The creditor uses the term as a euphemism.

68. *-erhéyt* is a fairly productive adverbializing suffix appendable to adjective roots: *naketerhéyt* 'nakedly,' *shtilerhéyt* 'quietly,' *lebedikerhéyt* 'while alive,' etc.

Instead of *gezunterhéyt*, the shorter form *gezúnt* may also occur adverbially in these blessings:

(89a) *Shlof gezúnt, shtey uf gezúnt, un zay gezúnt.* ("Sleep in good health, get up in good health, and be well.")

This is said to a child or other loved one as he is going to bed for the night.

While on the subject of formulas used when going to bed, we may note that in Yiddish one does not usually wish people pleasant dreams, though many other languages have such expressions (Greek *oneira glyka*, Turkish *tatlı rüyalar*, etc.).

69. *Es gezunterhéyt* may also be used to a person who is eating to spare him any possible embarrassment caused by the arrival of others who are not about to eat. Hebrew *beteyavon* ("with appetite!") and

Greek *kali orexi* ("good appetite!") may also function in this way.

70. A frequent variant of this blessing is:

(92a) *Tseráys es gezunterhéyt!* ("Tear it in good health!," i.e. "May you outlast this garment!")

Joseph Malone tells me that an exactly similar expression is used in Irish: *Go mairir agus go gcaithir é* "May you live to wear it out."

   In Greek one says *me gheia* 'with health' to someone wearing a new garment, and in Turkish *güle güle giy* 'wear [it] laughingly.' The similarity between Yiddish *gezunterhéyt* and Turkish *güle güle* was noted already in Zimmer 1958. See above, note 31.

71. There is an exact Turkish equivalent here: *güle güle git, güle güle gel* (*gitmek* 'go,' *gelmek* 'come').

   It has been suggested that *Gay gezunterhéyt* might make a good motto for the Healthy Hebrew Homophile Organization.

72. As always, one may use *gezunterhéyt* ironically, as in the following example (provided by Norval Slobin):

(93b) *Meyle, der meshúgener hot zikh aléyn dershosn, gezunterhéyt.* ("Well, the crazy fool shot himself, and good riddance!")

73. The noun *shver* 'father-in-law' is homophonous with the adjective or adverb *shver* 'difficult, tough.' Thus if one leaves out the intonational pause after the first word of (94), an allo-malo-petitive expression results:

(94a) *Shver lebn zolt ir.* ("May you live in difficulty.")

Thanks to Herbert Paper for pointing this out.

74. *Kadesh* is the name of a prayer that a son recites for his dead parent. By extension a man may refer to his son as *mayn kadesh* 'he who will say *kadesh* for me some day.' 120 years is the proverbial longest span of life that one can reasonably expect.

75. The pronoun may certainly be inserted (*zol er/zi gezúnt zayn; zoln zey gezúnt zayn*), though this makes the expression sound less

parenthetical, since it could now stand as a complete utterance by itself.

76.   The writer wishes to dissociate himself from the chauvinistic sentiments expressed in this example.

77.   Abbreviated from RP, pp. 12-13.

78.   Joe Malone observes that the same sort of palliative blessings are used in Irish.   He quotes the following excerpt from a letter to the Irish magazine *Feasta* (January 1969), written by a certain Deasún Breatnach as part of an ongoing scholarly debate with one L. S. Gógan:

> *"An rud is mó faoin Ghóganach, <u>bail ó Dhia air,</u> a chuireann díomá orm is é nach mbacann sé le húdarás a thabhairt faoi rud ar bith a deir sé."* ("The thing which most annoys me about Gógan, *the prosperity of God be upon him*, is that he doesn't bother to cite authorities for anything he says.")

79.   One should pronounce a blessing upon arising in the morning, eating or drinking anything, washing the hands, smelling something nice, putting on a new garment, etc.   The legal requirements for these blessings were first codified in the fourth tractate of the Mishna, around the second century A.D.

80.   These Hebrew words are given in the 'Ashkenazic' pronunciation, the one used by Yiddish speakers in Eastern Europe (as opposed to the 'Sephardic' pronunciation now used in Israel).   The word *borúkh* also appears in the formula of gratitude *borkhashém* discussed in section 3.0.

81.   Such a study is far beyond the present writer's area of competence.

82.   The expression may be malo-petitive just as well: 'He should only drop dead!'   'Amen!'   By extension, one may speak of an *oméyn-zoger* (lit. 'amen-sayer'), that is, a yes-man, somebody who only confirms what others have said, but never says anything original on his ow

83. For a very funny use of this expression as a response to a *malo-petitive* utterance see sentence (315). Tannen reports an identical Greek formula: *ap' to stoma sou kai stou Theou t'afti.*

84. Notice the beautiful consonant cluster -ntšstz- (although morpheme and word boundaries intervene, of course).

85. This is very similar to the encouraging Greek expression used to an unmarried woman of marriageable age who is attending somebody else's wedding: *kai sta dhika sou* 'and at yours!' (Tannen and Öztek, [44].)

86. The malo-fugitive equivalent of this proverb is:

   (113a) *Zol zikh dos azóy nit trefn vi es treft zikh.* ("Would that things would not happen the way they do happen.")
See section 7.

87. Zelda Kahan has supplied me with an even more innocent version:

   (117a) *Oyb mayn bobe volt gevén mayn zeyde, volt mayn zeyde gevén mayn bobe.* ("If my grandmother had been my grandfather, my grandfather would've been my grandmother.")

88. Karl Zimmer quotes a close German equivalent upon which this Yiddish variant may have been calqued: *Wenn die Grossmutter Räder hätte, wäre sie ein Fahrrad.* ("If grandmother had wheels, she'd be a bicycle.")

89. One more, from Herbert Paper:

   (119a) *Ven di bobe volt gehát vos der zeyde hot, volt zi gedavnt baym nomen/omud.* ("If grandmother had had what grandfather has, she would have prayed at the Holy Ark.")

Dávenen baym nomen (lit. "praying at the [Holy] name") or *dávenen baym omud* (lit. "praying [while] standing [before the Holy Ark]") refers to the most prestigious honor that can be paid in the synagogue to a male lay member of the congregation, when he is called up to the *bime* platform to pray before the open Ark.

90. It is, I think, meaningless to try to decide which of these psychic attitudes is 'more basic.' Each implies the other. When you bless someone you are 'getting there first,' before evil has a chance to strike. When you shun evil, you are clinging to the good lest it be taken away from you.

91. *Apotropaism* is defined as 'the use of magic and ritualistic ceremony to anticipate and prevent evil.'

92. We cannot undertake a serious study of Yiddish euphemisms here. They are of several types, not all of which are directly malo-fugitive The reluctance to mention certain words for God out of proper religi-ous context is undoubtedly malo-fugitive in origin (to pronounce a taboo name for God might provoke divine retribution), though it has been overlaid with other sentiments which obscure the issue. For some discussion of euphemism as a device to foil evil spirits, see 7.5 below. For euphemism as a method of legitimating malo-petition or cursing, see 9.5 below.

Related to euphemism, but distinct from it, is the pervasive rhetorical device of *irony*. Saying the opposite of what you mean is euphemistic if the intent is malo-fugitive; it is ironic if the intent is merely humorous or sarcastic.

Yiddish humor is preeminently ironic. Almost all psycho-osten-sives may be manipulated for ironic effect [see the use of *gezunter-héyt* in (93b), of *kholile* in (146), of *nebekh* in (38), etc.].

93. One is reminded of the ancient symbol of the three monkeys -- see no evil, speak no evil, hear no evil.

94. The word for 'not' has two free variants for most Yiddish speak-ers, *nit* and *nisht*. The NP in this expression receives contrastive stress -- 'may it be unthinkable in *your* case!'

95. There is also a Hebrew-derived formula available for this func-tion: *loy aleykhem* 'not to you [am I applying this odious term]':

(125a) *Der yíngerer [bruder] iz gevén, loy aleykhem, a shoyte.*
("The younger [brother] was -- and I don't mean you -- a fool."
L'Chayim, p. 84.)

This example illustrates what Tannen and Öztek call the *rapport estab-lishment* function of formulaic expressions. The situation in (125a) is the mirror image of the 'praising one friend in the presence of another' scene that calls for the Turkish formula *sizden iyi olmasın* 'may he/she not be better than you' (Tannen and Öztek, ex. 22).

Other Yiddish psycho-ostensives that seem to serve primarily a rapport establishment function are the *palliative blessings* discussed above (6.3).

96. Cf. the English expression 'I wouldn't wish it on my worst ene-my,' and Turkish *Allah düşmanıma vermesin* 'may God not give [even] to my enemy' (Tannen and Öztek, Turkish Appendix, No. 121).

This Yiddish construction may also be used in a temporal con-text, by filling the NP slot with *haynt* 'today' (*nisht far haynt gedakht*). This is appropriate when mentioning an unpleasant event that took place in the past:

(125b) *Un azóy iz dos gevén in der milkhome, nisht far haynt gedákht.* ("And that's the way it was during the war -- may it be unthinkable for today.")

97. This could mean either that the speaker hopes his hearer will never himself get sick, or that he hopes his hearer will never have *his* wife get sick on him.

98. This is the origin of the expression *you shouldn't know from it* that one finds in Yiddish-influenced American English.

99. It is related to the stem *khalel* 'desecrate; ruin; make unfit.' Cf. such expressions as *khilul ha-shem* 'blasphemy,' *khilul shabes* 'desecrating the Sabbath,' etc.

Zelda Kahan points out that the first occurrence of *kholile* in the Bible is in Genesis 18:25 (*kholilo lekho me-asos ka-dovor haze* 'It is unthinkable for you to do this' -- said by Abraham to God, who is contemplating the destruction of Sodom and Gomorrah).

In one interesting passage (Jeremiah 31:5) a verb *khalel* occurs with a meaning that remains rather obscure: *noteu noyteim ve-khileylu* 'the planters shall plant, and shall eat [them] as common things' (King James translation; here the verb is identified with *khol* 'sand; common thing'). The Revised Standard Version has a completely different interpretation: 'the planters shall plant, and shall enjoy the fruit.'

100. We conventionally translate *kholile* by '--horrors!--.' Note, however, that no intonational pause marks the word off from the rest of its sentence in the Yiddish original. It is usually absorbed smoothly into the flow of its sentence, receiving if anything a lower pitch than the surrounding words, in a manner typical of parenthetical expressions in general.

101. The use of *kholile* in non-first person sentences requires a certain empathic attitude by the speaker. The speaker is reporting what he feels the abhorrence of the actual person involved must have been.

102. The reference is to the proverbial expression 'Money is round,' i.e. it can slip through your fingers all too easily, just as a coin can roll away from you.

103. Note that in this sentence *kholile* is inserted *after* the stigmatized event. In cases like this, it *is* set off from the neighboring material by intonational pauses, since it is a kind of after-thought.

104. These sentences fairly drip with sarcasm. Not only do we have *kholile*, but also the expressions *a bisele* 'a tiny bit' and *a kapetshke* 'a weensy drop,' which, while appearing to minimize the fault, actually make it stand out the more.

105. Cf. Rosten, *op cit.*, p. 88.

106. Actually in sentences (150) and (152), the question preceding the *kholile* is not raised by the speaker himself, but merely echoed

after someone else had raised it. We have seen above (107) that a 'silly question' may alternatively elicit a *palliative blessing.*

107. In this example the malo-fugition is accentuated by the following allo-malo-petitive formula. The idea is, may the notion of sickness be dispelled from us and cleave instead to our enemies. See the discussion of scapegoats, section 7.6.

108. My colleague Ariel Bloch surmises that *khas* derives from the Hebrew stem *khus* 'pity.' The meaning of *sholem*, of course, is 'peace.' So *khas-ve-sholem* probably means something like 'May we have divine mercy and peace (instead of this horrible event that has been mentioned)!'

Zelda Kahan points out that *khas-ve-sholem* does not appear in the Bible as a set phrase, though the word *khus* occurs with *ayin* 'eye' in the expression *lokhus ayin* 'to take pity' (*lo tokhus ayin eylov* 'Don't take pity on him,' Deut. 19:13), as well as by itself (*ato khasto al ha-kikoyoyn* 'You took pity on [had empathy for] the cactus,' Jonah 4:10).

109. A close Greek equivalent of *Got zol ophitn* is *Theos fylaxi* 'God protect!' (Tannen and Öztek, Ex. 36).

110. This sentence defies a closely literal translation, since in English we cannot have an optative clause embedded in an adverbial clause of degree: *as stingy as may God guard and save us from.* This is a common Yiddish device for intensifying unpleasant adjectives:

(160a) *Es iz gevén a fróstiker víntertog, kalt, az zol zikh eyn Got derbáremen.* ("It was a frosty winter's day, cold -- as may God pity us [and spare us from]." *L'Chayim,* p. 94.)

111. Clearly, 'deflecting evil' is closely related to 'protecting from evil' [see section 7.3a]. There is merely a slight difference of emphasis: God protects *people* from evil, but deflects *evil* from people.

112. All peoples try to capture the infinite aspects of God's na-

ture by predicating a large variety of verbs to describe His divine
activities. We have seen that the God of Israel 'protects,' 'is merciful,' and 'forbids' (*inter alia*). In Lahu animist prayers the
Celestial Spirit *g̈ɨ̀-fū* simultaneously does all of the following:

> *fɨ̄* 'separates (men from misfortune),' *pâʔ* 'ordains,'
>
> *kɛ̄* 'purifies,' *ni* 'looks after,' *tɔ̂* 'is mindful of,'
>
> *šɨ̌* 'turns aside (misfortune),' *pò* 'saves,'
>
> *šu* 'withdraws (evils),' *lō* 'sees to the wants of,'
>
> *hàʔ-šá* 'cares for,' *hō* 'covers (with benevolence),'
>
> *qa* 'bestows,' etc.

See Anthony R. Walker, 1970a,b.

113. See section 3.0, especially the discussion of sentences (4)
and (14). A religious Jew (like a devout Buddhist who believes in
karma), realizes that God has His hidden reasons, and that an apparent
evil may be a blessing in disguise.

114. In Greek one can express gratitude that a bad event in the past
was not even worse by saying *mi cheirotera* 'not worse' (Tannen and
Öztek, Ex. 27). In Turkish one says *Allah beterinden saklasın* 'God
protect from worse' (*ibid.*, Ex. 26) or *Allah başka keder vermesin* 'may
God not give other grief' (*ibid.*, Turkish Appendix No. 77).

115. One is reminded of the saying 'I cried because I had no shoes --
until I saw a man who had no feet.'

A similar sentiment underlies King Lear's bitter realization that
one can never be so miserable that things might not get even worse:

> Oh, reason not the need. Our basest beggars
> Are in the poorest thing superfluous. [Act II, Sc. 4: 267-8]

116. I.e., the new one might be even worse than the old one. (Say,
maybe good old Lyndon Johnson wasn't so bad after all!)

117. From this attitude of 'evil-acceptance to avoid worse evil' it
is but a step to the *scapegoat* ploy [*section 7.6*]. We can say that
the evil we are now suffering and cheerfully accepting is a kind of

guarantee that nothing worse will follow. Thus if our best china vase
has just been smashed, we may say:

(191a) *Oyb es iz undz bashért tsores oder shlekhts, zol dos beser*
oysgeyn tsu der vaze. ("If we are fated to suffer trouble or evil,
may it rather go out into the vase [than into us]!")

   In Turkish when someone breaks or loses something, you hasten
to restore his perspective by saying *canın sağ olsun* 'may your soul
be alive' (Tannen and Öztek, Tk. App. No. 60).

118. For many speakers, the words *me vet* 'one will,' already reduced from *men vet*, are further elided into [mət], so that the tele-
scoped form becomes homophonous with *mit* 'with.' Thus, [a mət lebn]
could be folk-etymologized as meaning 'if [we are] with life.'

119. Greek and Turkish both abound in formulas to be used when dis-
cussing future plans: Gk. *o Theos voithos* 'God the helper' (Tannen
and Öztek, Gk. App. No. 32), *prota o Theos* 'God first' (*ibid.*, Ex.32);
Tk. *evel Allah* 'God first' (*ibid.*, Ex. 31), *inşallah* 'if God will'
(< Arabic), *Allah'ın izniyle* 'with God's permission' (*ibid.*, Tk. App.
No. 101), *Allah izin verirse* 'God permitting' (*ibid.*, Tk. App.
No. 102), and *Allah nasip ederse* 'if God gives [me my] share' (*ibid.*,
Tk. App. No. 109).

120. These spirits served a definite theological function. If the
arbitrary evils of this world could be attributed to their malevo-
lence, then the hands of God would be clean. All the good in the
world would derive from Him, but the evil could come from a different
source. If the Devil did not exist, it would have been necessary to
invent him.

121. Belief in evil spirits is much more pervasive among the Lahu
than among Jews, but for the Lahu too the spirits are conceived of
as powerful but stupid , easily deceived by simple magic devices.
Cf. Anthony R. Walker 1970a and Matisoff 1978b.

122. The asterisk in parentheses here is not meant to indicate that

the sentence is ungrammatical, only that it is wildly innappropriate in
this particular sociolinguistic context.

Actually the belief in demons who pounce on humans who boast of
their good fortune was by no means confined to the East European
peasantry, but seems also to be rooted in ancient Jewish tradition
itself. Cf. the Hebrew-derived admonition *al tiftakh pe le-sotn*
'Don't open your mouth to the Devil,' i.e. don't say anything that
might give the devil an excuse to strike.

123. A similar motivation underlies the practice of negating each
numeral one uses in counting something precious. Thus a busy mother
checking to see whether all her children were present would count
this way, pointing to each of them in turn:

> *Nit eyns, nit tsvey, nit dray, nit fir -- ale fir kinder zaynen
> nitó!* ("Not one, not two, not three, not four -- all four chil-
> dren aren't here.")

The idea seems to be that counting one's children directly is tanta-
mount to bragging of one's good fortune, and exposes one to the envy
of the spirits. Cf. the ancient Greek myth about Niobe, vainglorious
mother of seven sons and seven daughters, who incurred the wrath of
the goddess Leto who only had one of each. But Leto's children happened to be Apollo and Artemis! At their mother's bidding, they shot
all fourteen of Niobe's brood dead with arrows. See also sentence
(279) below.

124. The negative article *keyn* already negates the noun, but it is
possible to add the adverb *nit* or *nisht* 'not' for further emphasis.
One may also say *on ayn-hore* 'without evil eye.'

Belief in the Evil Eye is surprisingly widespread throughout
Europe and the Near East. In Irish, according to Joe Malone, the
Evil Eye goes by at least three names: *drochshúil* 'the bad eye,'
súil throm 'the heavy eye,' and *súil chiorrbhuighthe* 'the eye of destruction.'

In Greek the mention of a happy event or state is accompanied by a formula like *na mi vaskathis* 'may you not be touched by the evil eye' (Tannen and Öztek, Ex. 25), and in Turkish by *Allah nazardan saklasın* 'may God protect from the evil eye' (*ibid.*, Ex. 24) or *nazar değmesin* 'may the evil eye not touch you' (*ibid.*, Tk. App. No. 43).

125. An indication of the vitality of the Evil Eye concept in Jewish culture is the fact that *on ayn-hore* (note 124) has now been calqued back into modern Israeli Hebrew in the form *bli ayin raa* 'without an evil eye.'

There has been in fact a strong Israeli tendency to create new Hebrew psycho-ostensives modelled on Yiddish ones (see Note 58). This fits in well with Zimmer's and Tannen/Öztek's observations about the strange attractiveness of these formulas to those whose native languages lack them. See section 12.0, below.

126. In the speech of American Jews whose knowledge of Yiddish is imperfect, this formula is often thrown into an English sentence in an Anglicized version with final *-iy* instead of *-e*: [kənəhóriy]. This is a usual development in 'Yinglish' -- cf. [mátsiy] for *matse* 'matzo,' etc. Rosten reports a further corruption of the expression to 'canary,' as in 'Don't give me a canary!' Presumably users of this variant know practically no Yiddish at all, or else are being funny. At any rate they are spiritually far removed from their Eastern European cultural origins.

127. One is reminded of the hoary joke about the sadist and the masochist. The masochist says to the sadist, 'Hit me!' The sadist smiles subtly and replies, 'I will not!'

128. This point had already been made cogently by Zimmer (1958), who observed, "While in many situations speech is the marked member of the opposition *silence:speech*, in the situations requiring situational formulas it is rather silence which is the marked member of the opposition."

129. When merely *referring* to the phenomenon of the evil eye (as opposed to actually 'combatting' it in a formula), the speaker may

prefer to use the euphemistic expression *dos gut oyg* 'the good eye').
See section 7.1.

130. The notion of *evil hour* vs. *good hour* seems also to be pan-
European/Near Eastern, at least.

The first verse of the well-known Russian folksong *Ochi Chornye*
'Dark Eyes' ends:

... *uvidel vas ja v nedobryj chas* ("I [first] laid eyes on you in
an evil hour").

In Greek, when a fortunate event is mentioned, one adds the formula *i ora i kali* 'the good hour' or *ora kali* 'good hour' (Tannen and
Öztek, Gk. App. Nos. 25, 33).

131. According to Herbert Paper (pers. comm. 1973), there are exact
equivalents of this particular incantation in Polish and Russian.

132. Again there are exact equivalents in Greek (*vangase tin glossa
sou* 'bite your tongue' [Tannen and Öztek, Ex. 38]) and Turkish (*dilini
ısır* [*ibid.*, Tk. App. No. 143]). 'In the case of the Greek expression
one must actually close the teeth visibly on the tongue before the
conversation can proceed.'

One may also say in Turkish, when this situation arises, *ağzından
yel alsın* 'may the wind take it from your mouth' [*ibid.*, Ex. 37].

133. Actually there is no need to expectorate real saliva. It is
sufficient to avert one's head, make spitting movements of the lips,
and say *Pu, pu, pu!* .

134. Some actions of this type have startling uniformity across
cultures. In Greek, when something fortunate is mentioned, one may
say *ktypa xylo* 'knock wood' (Tannen and Öztek, Gk. App. No. 48),
just as millions of Americans still do.

135. Nowadays most people prefer to substitute for the bird a sum of
money, which is donated to charity. The original ritual with the
chicken is still performed by very orthodox Jews, especially in
Israel.

136.   More specifically, one can also refer to the human victim of a misfortune as a *kapore-hindl*.

In ordinary non-religious language the phrase *oyf kapores* 'as an expiation' has come to mean 'something expendable, something one would be willing to sacrifice,' as in the following idioms: *toygn oyf kapores* 'be good-for-nothing, useless;' *darfn oyf kapores* 'have no use for, need like a hole in the head;' *hobn oyf kapores* 'not give a fig for, not care a damn about.'

137.   Alternatively one could use *kapore* to refer to the victim rather than the event, and say:

(197a)   *Zol er zayn di kapore far mir!*   ("May he be the scapegoat for me!")

138.   In a humorous vein one can use the expression *di kapore vern far X* 'become the expiation for X' to mean 'fall in love with X; get a crush on X,' i.e. 'offer oneself as a willing victim for X's charms.' This is connected with the idea of self-immolation discussed immediately below.

139.   It is of course possible to turn around somebody else's curse so that it bounces back onto the curser:

(197b)   *Zol dos ónkumen tsu ale goyim, vos zey hobn dortn óngevuntshn dem hunt un dem yidn.*   ("May it befall all the Gentiles, what they there wished on the dog and the Jew!" *L'Chayim*, p. 93.)

This is a kind of retaliatory scape-goatism, of the type children use when they chant 'Everything you say goes right back to you!'

140.   This is a true story. The expression *for mir iber mitn trok* was proverbial in the author's parental home.

141.   From the words to the perennially popular music-hall hit *A Yídishe Mame* (New York, circa 1925).

142.   According to Zelda Kahan, the practice of using psycho-ostensives that bless the dead arose in the early centuries of the Christian era under the influence of learned commentaries on

Proverbs 10:7, which reads: *zeykher tsadik livrokho, vešem rešoim yirkov* ('The memory of the righteous man is a blessing, but the name of evildoers will perish').

Yiddish speakers are under particualr compulsion to use these expressions when the dead person in question had some close connection with the life of the speaker. The mention of a dead non-Jew is usually allowed to pass without comment, especially if he is long dead. One does not say,

(*) Jean-Jacques Rousseau, may he rest in peace, was a precursor of romanticism.

An exception is certain notorious evil-doers of history, like Haman or Hitler, the mention of whose name may be accompanied by a curse. *See section 8.0d.*

143. Note that the speaker, when referring to his own death, takes care to place it 120 years in the future, the proverbial longest span of human life. *See section 6.3, note 74 .*

144. This is similar in flavor to Turkish *toprağı bol olsun* 'may his earth be plenty' (Tannen and Öztek, Tk. App. No. 103).

145. The idea of a paradisiacal afterlife is not much stressed in Judaism, compared to Christianity. The word *gan-eydn* is from Heb. 'Garden of Eden.'

The radiance of paradise is also invoked in the much more literal formula *neyroy yoir* 'may his light shine' (< Heb.), as well as in the Turkish *nur içinde yatsın* 'may he rest in holy light' (Tannen and Öztek, Tk. App. No. 97). The word *nur* 'light' (< Arabic) is cognate to Hebrew *neyr*.

146. Herbert Paper mentions another mortuo-bono-petitive expression involving paradise: *nukhoy eydn* "may his rest be (in) Eden" (< Heb.). Paper also cites the initials t-n-ts-b-h (pronounced /tənátsba/), which regularly appear on tombstones after the name of the deceased, standing for the Hebrew words "*tehi nishmosoy/nishmoso tsruro bitsroyr ha-khayim*" ("May his/her soul be bound up in the bonds of life.").

Rabbinical Hebrew (like modern Indonesian -- see Bruyns 1970) is in fact inordinately fond of acronyms. Sometimes these have a clear mnemonic value, as with the abbreviation found in the Passover Haggadah for the Ten Plagues which God visited upon the Egyptians (*datsakh adash beakhav*), short for *dom* 'blood,' *tsefardeye* 'frogs,' *kinim* 'lice,' etc.

Sometimes the acronym is used simply to save space, e.g. *zal* (for *zikhroyne livrokho*, esp. on tombstones), or *shlito* (for *sheyikhye leyomim toyvim arukhim* 'may he live good long days; may he have a long and good life' (< Heb.), usable after a name in the salutation or address of a letter).

Naturally this acronymic propensity lends itself to humorous manipulation. One way to insult somebody while pretending to praise him is to call him a *groyser poyel tsedek* 'great doer of righteousness.' Everyone will understand that the last two words are to be taken acronymically as a euphemism for *pots*, one of the most vulgar Yiddish terms of abuse.

147. A very similar expression containing *skhus* 'merit' is *zayn skhus zol mir bayshteyn* 'may his merit stand by me.'

148. Instead of *guter beter* one may use the Hebrew-derived expression *meylets yoysher* 'righteous intercessor:'

(211c) *Zay a meylets yoysher far mayn kind.* ("Be a righteous intercessor for my child.")

Meylits is used in modern Hebrew to mean 'interpreter.'

149. In Lahu animist religion, someone who has died an 'evil death' (*šɨ mâ dàʔ ve*), like an accident victim, or a woman who died in childbirth, is thought to harbor resentment toward the living, and must be propitiated lest he do grave harm to his surviving relatives and friends. See Anthony Walker, 1970a.

150. Another possible apologetic formula here is *mayn vort zol im nit tsu shver zayn* 'may my word(s) not be too hard for him.'

In Greek one can say *Theos schores'ton* 'God forgive him' (Tannen

and Öztek, Gk. App. No. 24) at the mention of any dead person, vir-
tuous or not. After all, the best of us are in need of divine for-
giveness for our shortcomings.

In Turkish the formula *Allah affetsin* 'may God forgive' is used
at the mention of any sinful person, dead or alive.

151. Herbert Paper cites a malo-petitive parody of the bono-petitive
olevasholem discussed above (8.0a). When speaking of the late un-
lamented czar, somebody hastened to add with mock respect *olov
ha-shnobl* 'may the beak be upon him' (with the Germanic-derived *shnobl*
'beak; spout; prow' substituting for the Hebrew-derived *sholem*
'peace').

152. This latter formula may also be used of living enemies. See
sentence (ii) about Governor Reagan in section 1.0.

153. Without the prefix, *vertlen zikh* means 'to joke around, make
witty remarks.' A *vertl* or *gláykhvertl* means a 'clever saying,
wisecrack, aphorism.' *Vertl* is of course the diminutive of *vort*
'word.'

154. A semi-humorous variant of *zidlen* is *zidlen un shnidlen,* where
the reduplicated verb is preceded by the productive, pejorative prefix
shm-. This complicated morphological process, involving reduplica-
tion, prefixation, and deletion of the underlying initial consonant
of the reduplicated syllable, is another of the gifts of Yiddish to
general American English (*culture-shmulture; friend-shmiend,* etc.).

155. The interested reader is urged to consult Rosten, *op. cit.,*
where some of the more common (and more obscene) ones are to be found.
The compilation of a scientific glossary of Yiddish verbal abuse is
long overdue.

Reinhold A. Aman, the leading American specialist in verbal
abuse, is now engaged in such a project, a task he has already
accomplished for Bavarian and Austrian German (see Aman 1973).

Drummond and Perkins 1973 is an excellent and accurate collection of Russian malo-petitives.

156. The expression *geyn iber di hayzer*, lit. 'go across/over the houses' refers to the common practice of seeking alms from door to door in the *shtetlekh* of Eastern Europe.

157. The verb *farginen*, like its German cognate *vergönnen*, means 'not to begrudge; not to envy good fortune.' When negated (*nit farginen, nicht vergönnen*), the meaning corresponds to the English non-negated verb 'begrudge.' A curious instance of non-parallel segmentations of semantic space.

158. A similar expletive with *ale* 'all' is *ale beyze khaloymes*, lit. 'all bad dreams:'

(226a) *Ale beyze khaloymes! Bistu meshuge?* ("All bad dreams! Are you crazy?" RP, p. 95.)

159. I.e. a knife suitable for use only with milk-products, according to the laws of *kashruth*. Note the repetition of the first part of the sentence as a tag at the end, with inverted subject and verb. This is common in emotional speech, and is a feature of the English of people under Yiddish influence: *He gave me the wrong one, he gave me!*

160. See 'humiliating imperatives,' section 9.5.

161. The idiom *hakn + Dative Noun + a tshaynik* (lit. 'to bang on a tea-kettle to Dative Noun'), meaning 'to yack away endlessly and re-morselessly at somebody about matters of no interest,' is familiar to most American Jews, no matter how little Yiddish they may know. In my family it is commonly inserted into English sentences like: *What are you hucking me a chainik about!*; *She hucked* /hʌkt/ *me such a chainik I felt like gagging her*. Notice that the vowel of the Yiddish *hakn* is preserved in the /ʌ/ of *hucked*, rather than substituting the semantically and etymologically related *hacked* /hækt/.

Irene Eber reports the 'Galitsianer' variant *hakn in tshaynik.*

162. For more on Yiddish euphemisms, see sections 7.1 and 9.5. Note that in this one expression, where 'good year' appears with the definite article, *yor* is construed as masculine instead of neuter

(one would expect **dos gute yor*). This grammatical peculiarity
(which seems to be most current in NE Yiddish) serves to mark this
expression as meaning something idiomatically different from the
overt meanings of its constituents.

163.   The Turkish formula *düşman başına* 'to enemy's head' (Tannen and
Öztek, Tk. App. 140) is used at the mention of something very bad.
It is therefore simultaneously auto-malo-fugitive and allo-malo-
petitive.   This shows the same psychosemantic dynamics as the *scapegoat* strategy discussed above (7.6).

164.   The animist Lahu recognize several distinct categories of evil
spirits, among which is one that 'bites' you from the outside (*nê
chè? ve*) and another which enters you so that you are 'possessed'
(*nê gɛ ve*).   See Walker 1970a and Telford 1937.

165.   This is a common gambit of cursers the world over.   Cf. English
'son of a bitch,' etc.

166.   In RP, a whole joke (No. 9, p.8) revolves around the incongruous use of this expression with the polite second person pronominal
adjective *ayer* instead of the familiar *dayn*.

167.   Cholera seems always to have held a special terror for the
Jews.   In the Middle Ages the name of the disease was folk-etymologized into Hebrew as *kholi-ra* 'the evil disease.'   (The *ra* is the
same morpheme as in *ayn-hore* 'evil eye.').   The widespread panic
that swept the Israeli population in 1970 when some cases of cholera
broke out in Old Jerusalem attests to the continuing dread felt
towards that awesome disease.

The Yiddish pronunciation of the word varies (*kholerye* ~
kholyere ~ *kholyerye*); that is, either or both of the liquids may be
palatalized.

168.   Some morbid conditions are expressed by means of verbs rather
than nouns in these curses, notably *rinen* 'run (as a sore),
suppurate' (*zol im rinen fun di oygn* 'May his eyes run!'); and
shveln or *ónshveln* 'swell up,' usually in the past passive participial

form, *geshvoln vern* or *óngeshvoln vern* 'be swollen.' We may symbolize such verbs by V_d, for 'verbs of disease.'

169. Proverbial expressions meaning 'to receive nothing at all of value' are *krign a krenk* ('receive a disease') and *krign kadokhes* ('receive malaria'). A crude way of refusing to give someone anything is:

(241a) *Gebn dir a krenk!* ("I'll give you a disease [instead of what you asked for]!")

170. The verb *péygern* is used outside of curses only for the death of animals. Hence 'like a dog' in the English gloss. The variant where the main verb precedes the auxiliary is somewhat more emphatic. Cf. the expressions relating to modes of being killed, *below*.

171. Note that one can include a dative first-person pronoun here. This is a kind of 'ethical dative:' *Go to hell for me, will you!*

172. Passive participles are formed in Yiddish by combining the past participle of the main verb with the auxiliary *vern* 'become.' [See note 168].

Sometimes the curse calls for a continuing process of suffering rather than a clean death. In these cases *vern* cannot be used:

(262a) *Un beshás zi iz gevén a yunge meydl, hot men ir gerédt a shidekh mit Aleksander dem dritn, brotn zol er zikh afn fayer.* ("And when she was a young girl, they arranged a marriage for her with Alexander III, may he roast in flames." *L'Chayim*, p. 140.)

173. As a cover term for all sorts of strange or violent deaths, one may use the expression *mise meshune* (< Heb. 'different death; death out of the ordinary'):

(269a) *A mise meshune zol er hobn!* ("May he have an abnormal death!")

This is a concept similar to the Lahu *ší mâ dà? ve* (See note 149).

174. I am indebted to Norval Slobin for this example.

175.   Actually the verb does not appear at all on the surface in this sentence. Cf. the pro-verbal use of motion-adverbs like *aráyn* [*section 9.4c, above*]. This simple negation of the key word is the same psychosemantically as the negative way of counting one's children [*note 123, above*].

176.   Variants of this vegetable-curse are legion:

(281a)   *Es zoln im vaksn búrikes in boykh!* ("May beets grow in his belly!")

(281b)   *Zoln im vaksn búrikes in pupik, un zol er pishn mit borsht!* ("May beets grow in his belly-button and let him piss out borscht!")

The juicy collection of curses to be found in Singer 1977 contains mostly examples of this type (all in English, unfortunately -- there is not a single Yiddish word in the whole book). A single mild example will serve: 'May you marry the best cook in the world -- and get ulcers.'

The brilliant researches of Labov (e.g. 1972a) into the creative use of ritual insults among teenage urban blacks has opened up for us another culture where eloquence and virtuosity are considered essential for effective verbal abuse.

Distant echoes of this living tradition are felt even among white middle-class children who attend integrated public schools, as in Berkeley, where the kids startled us a few years ago by bringing home a chant that soon became a family favorite:

"Mm! Ngawa!
Your daddy need a shower
Your mama need a shave...
Your greasy granny got a hole in her pantie
got a big behin' like Frankenstein
goin' beep, beep, beep *down Sesame Street..."*

177.   Another watery insult in this vein is the very common *ikh hob dikh in bod* (lit. 'I have you in the bath'), probably a euphemism for

ikh hob dikh in drerd ('I have you in hell,' i.e. 'For all I care you can go to hell').

178. My father tells a story about a constipated old woman who re-plied to this particular curse with a sigh and the auto-bono-petitive exclamation: *Oy, haleváy volt ikh geként!* ("Oh, if only I could!"). See the discussion of *haleváy*, section 5.0b, above.

179. An exact Irish equivalent is *póg mo thón*, which is frequently used by Irish Americans with no knowledge of Irish at all. Joe Malone notes: "In my family, the received anglicization was [pòwgəməhówn], the Irish *Vorlage* being something like [po:gmɔho:n] in the Munster dialect."

180. This particular example I owe to a satirical revue called, I am sorry to say, 'Bagels and Yox,' to which I was taken in my early youth.

181. The expression *I need it like a hole in the head*, now apparently in general use in American English, seems certainly to be a direct translation of Yiddish *ikh darf es hobn azóy vi a lokh in kop*. Here too the speaker, by using a striking comparison, invites the hearer to make his own deduction: 'Does he need a hole in the head? Of course not. Therefore he really doesn't need *this* either.'

182. The same pattern may in fact be used auto-bono-petitively:

(289a) *Gey, nárele! Zol ikh hobn azóy fil tóyznter, vifl yidn es veln haynt esn!* ("Come on, silly! I should only have as many thousand[-ruble notes] as there will be Jews eating today [on Yom Kiper]!" *L'Chayim*, p. 61.)

183. The *Agrárfrage* -- whether, where, and how the Jews of Europe should resettle elsewhere in the world and become farmers -- was a burning issue among the intelligentsia of the turn of the century. The question received added importance after the Russian Revolution.

184. Adding further plausibility to the mistranslation is the phono-logical similarity between *imrosi* and the Hebrew word *imi* 'my mother'

(sometimes incorrectly rendered as *imosi* by Yiddish speakers with imperfect knowledge of Hebrew).

185. The technique is really to *presuppose* the correctness of each of the glosses in turn, so that the hearer will be momentarily confused into accepting still another false gloss, which then becomes eligible for being presupposed itself. Students of the logic of presupposition [*see section 1.0 above*] could do worse than to steep themselves in Yiddish humor.

For the presuppositions involved in swearing oaths, see the next section.

186. Quite similar in this respect are English oaths like *so help me God*, which really mean 'may God help me so.'

187. By *bono-petitive oath* I mean 'an oath whose appeal is bono-petitive.'

188. Swearing falsely, or 'bearing false witness,' is a violation of one of the Ten Commandments, and is thus a direct invitation for divine punishment. This of course does not stop some people from using oaths mendaciously. *See below*.

189. The stress falls on the subject pronoun, regardless of whether or not it is inverted with the auxiliary. There seems to be no discernible shade of emphasis distinguishing the two variants, though the non-inverted formula is more likely to occur as an independent utterance than parenthetically.

190. I used to think that 'I should live so!' or 'I should live so long!' were normal English expressions. My wife assures me that no WASP would ever use them. The idea of swearing by one's life, health, etc., strikes the typical American English speaker either as hopelessly archaic (like 'by my beard!' or 'God's wounds!') or as rather sentimentally foreign (like 'by the white hairs of my sainted mother'). What a WASP *can* swear by is the salvation of his soul (*I'll be damned if...*). See section 10.2.

191. Inversions are possible between *zayn* and *gezúnt* (*zol ikh azóy*

gezúnt zayn!), and/or between *ikh* and *zol.*

192. From the context in RP it is clear that this very emphatic oath is mendacious.

193. For a discussion of the concept of *nakhes*, see section 6.0.

194. For the concept of 'knowing of evil,' see section 7.1c.

195. Yiddish has a very tenuous distinction between long and short vowels, with the long vowels usually occurring in Hebrew-derived words with a 'weak' medial consonant (like *h, ?, ʕ*) that disappears intervocalically. Herbert Paper cites the following minimal pairs:

> *tsar* 'czar' / *tsaar* 'misery' (< Heb.)
>
> *bal* 'ball, dance' / *baal* 'the god Baal' (< Heb.)
>
> *kol* 'voice' (< Heb.) / *kool* 'congregation, community' (< Heb.
> *kohol*).

This distinction is extremely marginal, and disappears in rapid speech.

196. The formula *I'll be damned if...* is, in fact, the closest English equivalent to Yiddish auto-malo-petitive appeals. As in Yiddish, if the following proposition if overtly positive, the hearer interprets the meaning as negative. 'I'll be damned if I'll go!' means 'I swear I won't go.' Note, however, that in English, the converse also applies: if the following proposition is overtly negative, the hearer interprets the meaning as positive. Thus *I'll be damned if I won't go!* means 'I swear I will go!' But in Yiddish, the formula following a malo-petitive appeal cannot be overtly nega-tive. One cannot say:

 (306a) **Zol ikh azóy visn fun beyz, vi ikh veys nit, vos iz geshén.*
 ("So may I know of evil, the way I don't know what happened.")

to mean 'I swear I do know what happened.' A sentence like (306a) is uninterpretable.

197. There is one other auto-malo-petitive oath that survives in ordinary English: 'cross my heart and hope to die.' But nobody

uses this any more except children.

198. We may regard *nit* in the malo-fugitive appeal as *pleonastic* in quite the same sense as literary French *ne* in sentences like:

> *Je crains qu'il ne vienne* 'I fear he will come'; 'I fear lest he come.'

In both the Yiddish and the French cases the speaker inserts the negative morpheme as a reflection of his true underlying feelings (what he wants is *not* to know evil, or for him *not* to come), even though he thus seems to fly in the face of the propositional logic of the sentence.

That the *ne* in the French example is not filling its usual negative function is proven by the fact that it changes the meaning to add *pas* after the verb in the embedded clause.

199. One is reminded of the ancient riddle about the oracle. You are told that the oracle either speaks the truth all the time or lies all the time, but you don't know which. Then you ask him directly whether he is telling the truth ...

200. The branch of linguistics that concerns itself specifically with the *extra-linguistic situation* is now called *pragmatics* by many American linguists. The 'pragmatic' approach is now being applied to language acquisition studies with brilliant results. See Ochs, ed., *Developmental Pragmatics* (in press).

201. Tannen and Öztek (p. 517) contrast Yiddish to Greek and Turkish with respect to parenthesizability and variability, as follows: 'Yiddish psycho-ostensives, God bless them, are more often sentence-interruptors, and there is a priority in Yiddish culture on verbal inventiveness, so that these emotive expressions are productive. In contrast, Greek and Turkish formulas are a fixed set, and are, more often than not, complete utterances in themselves, although some do come in the middle of sentences.'

202. These relationships have nothing to do with 'hiding one's true feelings' or attempting to deceive someone else. Rather they are

organic connections inherent in the psychic states themselves. Conscious mendacity in the use of psycho-ostensives is quite another issue, which further complicates the picture. *See below.*

203. Tannen and Öztek discuss such a *continuum of obligatoriness*, observing that "Turkish has many formulas which cluster at the obligatory end of the continuum, while formulas in English tend towards the optional end. Greek has fewer fixed formulas than Turkish, but many more than English" (pp.516-7).

The Greek and Turkish formulas in the Appendices to Tannen and Öztek are ranked in descending order of obligatoriness, as determined empirically according to the judgments of 25 Athenian Greeks and 23 Turkish graduate students in California.

It is my feeling (based on two years' residence in Japan in six sojourns between 1960 and 1977) that the situational formulas of Japanese, incredibly multitudinous as they are, constitute a fixed set or closed class, and the Japanese speaker is not expected to invent new ones of his own (though of course he is free, like the Yiddish speaker, to manipulate them for humorous or ulterior purposes). There exist conservative etiquette books in Japanese running to several hundred pages containing lists of the proper formulas to use for all occasions, both epistolary and conversational. The formulas are rigidly fixed, even when the possible occasions of their use are relatively rare (e.g. formulas for consoling someone who has suffered damage in an earthquake). See, for example, Anonymous 1961.

204. Cf. the negative method of offering thanks (10); the negative way to curse a cat (279), etc.

205. For *kholerye* and *péygern*, see sections 9.3-4. For *from your mouth to God's ears*, which is normally used as an expression of assent to a blessing, see sentence (110). The three words *hunt, kelev,* and *sobake* all mean "dog" (< Germanic, Hebrew, and Russian, respectively).

206. No fewer than 21 proverbs in Ayalti's collection have to do with speech and silence.

207.   This is a parody of the famous Mishnaic verse: *Eyzehu giboyr?*
Ha-koyvesh es yitsroy.   ("Who is to be called mighty?   He who suppresseth his passion."   *Pirke Avoth* [Sayings of the Fathers],
Mishna Avoth 4:1.)   Thanks to Baruch Bokser for providing me chapter
and verse.

208.   A similar sentiment in a more lighthearted vein is expressed
by the saying

  (322a)   *Fun zogn nemt men nisht trogn.*   ("You don't get pregnant
  just by talking").

We may preserve the rhyme in English by the rather strained translation: *From being talked up you can't get knocked up.*

209.   'Something of an epilogue,' this section was added during the
final prepublication revision of this book in September, 1978.

210.   Compare for example the verbs of Russian, Chinese, Eskimo, and
Tagalog!

211.   For a study of how the languages of Southeast Asia are similar
to yet different from each other, see Matisoff 1978c.

212.   One familiar example is English *it goes without saying* (< French
ça va sans dire).

    The most complete and cogent treatment of language contact phe-
nomena available in English is still Weinreich 1953, one of that great
Yiddishist's most important contributions to general linguistics.

213.   For discussions of the criteria for deciding among these various
possibilities, see Matisoff 1976, 1978a.

214.   The adjectives *Sephardic* and *Ashkenazic* are from the medieval
Hebrew names for Spain and Germany, respectively.   The nouns for Jews
of each branch are *Sephardim, Ashkenazim* (plural), or *Sephardi,
Ashkenazi* (singular).

215.   By profession Schwartz is an Indo-Europeanist, specializing in
the languages of Iran, especially ancient Sogdian.   He is interested

in tracing cultural relationships through the Indo-Iranian area, Armenia, and the Levant. In his spare time, Schwartz has assembled what is undoubtedly California's largest collection of early Greek, Turkish, Armenian, and Jewish phonograph records.

216. The Greek city of Salonika (ancient Thessalonika) was one of the most thriving centers of Sephardic Jewish culture before World War II. The Jewish population of the city was exterminated with particular thoroughness by the Nazis.

217. Besides the large Sephardic community of Greek Jews who came originally from Spain or North Africa, there was another smaller group centered in the town of Ioannina, who were 'indigenous' inhabitants of Greece as far back as can be traced, perhaps even before the destruction of the Second Temple in A.D. 70. (Pers. comm., Rae Dalven.)

218. Schwartz thinks that Levantine music was spread to the Ashkenazic communities of Eastern Europe by itinerant Jewish musicians. The gypsies must also have played a role in this still mysterious story.

219. Speaking very roughly indeed, one can distinguish between the more hotblooded or funky Southern/Eastern European cultures, where emotionally charged psychic states are allowed relatively free linguistic expression, and the cooler, more reserved, stiff-upper-lip sort of Anglo-Saxon or Nordic culture, where greater emphasis is placed on controlling or suppressing the linguistic and paralinguistic expression of strong emotions like anger, fear, or grief. (Stereotypes do have a certain minimal validity, after all!).

220. Tannen and Öztek, ex. 42. A similar good wish is still offered to newlyweds in Italy: *figli maschi in quantità* 'male children in large numbers.'

221. Japanese formulas (like many Turkish ones [Tannen and Öztek, p. 520]) are highly sensitive to the relative social status of the participants in the speech act. One might almost call them *status-ostensive* more than psycho-ostensive.

222. My colleague Charles Fillmore and his students are now actively

engaged in collecting thousands of such English expressions.

223.   Zimmer, *op. cit.*, p. 7. The interactional quality of these utterances is, of course, most obvious in the case of *paired formulas*, where both parties to the speech act have something conventional to say. (E.g. Turkish *eline sağlık* 'health to your hand' [said by the eater to the cook], to which the cook must reply *afiyet olsun* 'bon appétit.').

224.   This entire exchange is a calque on the Greek paired formulas *kalos orises* (lit. 'it's good you came') / *kalos sas vrika* (lit. 'it's good I found you.'). (Tannen and Öztek, Gk. App. Nos. 7, 18).

225.   Psychosemantics in this sense is thus totally different from the established subdiscipline known as *psycholinguistics*, where the accent has mostly been on controlled and replicable experiments intended to prove the validity of generative grammar in the realm of language acquisition. For an early anthology illustrating this approach, see Saporta 1961.

226.   My favorite writer on animal behavior is Dr. Frank Miller, who writes a daily column called "The Wonderful World of Animals" in the San Francisco *Chronicle*.

227.   'Neurolinguistics' is approaching this from the physiological, experimental side, trying to localize particular speech functions in particular areas of the brain's tissue (e.g. nouns in one hemisphere and verbs in the other!). See Ornstein 1977.

228.   Erickson's successful therapeutic techniques, some of them verbal and others non-verbal, have been lucidly analyzed and entertainingly presented in Haley 1973. A less happy attempt at exegesis is Bandler and Grinder 1975, which takes a heavy-handed generative line.

229.   This is a potential goldmine of material for discourse analysts.

230.   See, e.g. Berne 1964.

231.   These correspond very roughly to the *id, ego,* and *superego* of Freudian psychology, though the *child* is viewed in much more positive terms (as the source of creative curiosity, etc.) than Freud viewed the *id.*

232.   When very relaxed or very excited (i.e. when the *inner child* is in command) I sometimes drop post-vocalic *-r,* a feature of my native Eastern Massachusetts dialect which never reappears otherwise.

233.   I.e., 'mind-expanding' (author's neologism).

BIBLIOGRAPHY

Aman, Reinhold A.   1973. *Bayrisch-österreichisches Schimpfwörterbuch*. München.

Anonymous. 1961. *Tegami, aisatsu yōgo jiten* [Dictionary of Phraseology for Letters and Greetings]. Jitsugyō no Nihonsha. Tokyo.

Ayalti, Hanan J., ed. 1949. Yiddish Proverbs. With six woodcuts by Bernard Reder. Translated from the Yiddish by Isidore Goldstick. First paperback edition, 1963. Schocken Books. New York.

Bailey, Charles-James N. and Roger W. Shuy, eds. 1973. New Ways of Analyzing Variation in English. Georgetown University Press. Washington D.C.

Bandler, Richard and John Grinder. 1975. Patterns of the Hypnotic Techniques of Milton H. Erickson, M.D. Volume I. Meta Publications. Cupertino, California.

Bastomski, Sh. 1920. *Baym kval: yídishe shpríkhverter, vertlekh, gláykhvertlekh, rédnsartn, farglaykhenishn, brokhes, víntshenishn, kloles, kharomes, simonim, sgules, zabóbones*. Naye Yídishe Folksshul. Vilna.

Berne, Eric. 1964. Games People Play: the Psychology of Human Relationships. Grove Press. New York.

Bernstein, Ignacy. 1969. *Jüdische Sprichwörter und Redensarten*. G. Olms. Hildesheim. [Translated by Gershon Weltman and Marvin S. Zuckerman as Yiddish Sayings Mama Never Taught You (1975). Perivale Press. Van Nuys, California.].

Birdwhistell, Ray L. 1970. Kinesics and Context: essays on body motion communication. University of Pennsylvania Press. Philadelphia.

Bloch, Chana Faerstein. 1969. "Peddling Yiddish." [Review of Rosten 1968, The Joys of Yiddish]. Midstream (March 1969), pp. 75-80.

Brichto, Herbert C. 1962. The Problem of 'Curse' in the Hebrew Bible University of Pennsylvania doctoral dissertation. Published 1963 by Society of Biblical Literature, Philadelphia. Reprinted with corrections 1968.

Bruyns, A. Mörzer. 1970. Glossary of Abbreviations and Acronyms Used in Indonesia. Djakarta.

Chafe, Wallace L. 1970. Meaning and the Structure of Language. University of Chicago Press. Chicago.

_____. 1973. "Language and memory." Language 49.2: 261-281.

_____. 1974. "Language and consciousness," Language 50.1:111-133.

Chomsky, Noam. 1957. Syntactic Structures. Mouton and Co. The Hague.

Colson, Elizabeth. 1973. "Tranquility for the decision maker." In Laura Nader and Thomas Maretzki, eds. Cultural Illness and Health. American Anthropological Association. Anthropological Study #9. Washington D.C.

Dahbany-Miraglia, Dina. 1975. "Verbal protective behavior among Yemenite Jews." Working Papers on Yiddish and East European Jewish Studies #13. YIVO Institute for Jewish Research. New York.

Drummond, D. A. and G. Perkins. 1973. A Short Dictionary of Russian Obscenities. 2nd, revised edition. Berkeley Slavic Specialties. Berkeley.

Feinsilver, Lillian Mermin. 1970. The Taste of Yiddish. Thomas Yoseloff, publisher. South Brunswick; New York; London.

Fillmore, Charles. 1971. "Verbs of judging: an exercise in semantic description." In C. Fillmore and D. T. Langendoen, eds. Studies in Linguistic Semantics. Holt, Rinehart, and Winston. New York.

Gevirtz, Stanley. 1960. Curse Motifs in the Old Testament and in the Ancient Near East. University of Chicago doctoral dissertation.

Goffman, Erving. 1959. The Presentation of Self in Everyday Life. Doubleday. Garden City, N.Y.

_____. 1969. Strategic Interaction. University of Pennsylvania Press. Philadelphia.

_____. 1974. Frame Analysis: an essay on the organization of experience. Harvard University Press. Cambridge, Mass.

Gross, Morris. 1935. The Relation of Blessing and Cursing in the
    Psalms to the Evolution of Hebrew Religion. University of Chicag
    doctoral dissertation.

Grunwald, Max. ed. *Mitteilungen zur jüdischen Volkskunde*. [32 volumes
    published until 1929]. [*Organ der Gesellschaft für jüdische
    Volkskunde (Hamburg) und der Gesellschaft für Sammlung und
    Konservierung von Kunst- und historischen Denkmälern des Judentum
    (Wien)*].

Haley, Jay. 1973. Uncommon Therapy. Norton. New York.

Herzog, Marvin I. 1965. The Yiddish Language in Northern Poland:
    its geography and history. Publication of the Indiana University
    Research Center in Anthropology, Folklore, and Linguistics, No. 3
    Bloomington, Indiana.

Herzog, Marvin I.; W. Ravid; and Uriel Weinreich, eds. 1969. The
    Field of Yiddish (III). Mouton and Co. The Hague.

Herzog, Marvin I.; Barbara Kirshenblatt-Gimblett; Dan Miron; and Ruth
    Wisse, eds. 1979. The Field of Yiddish: Studies in Language,
    Folklore, and Literature. Fourth Collection. ISHI Publications.
    Philadelphia.

Kirshenblatt-Gimblett, Barbara. 1974. "The concept and varieties of
    narrative performance in East European Jewish Culture." In
    Explorations in the Ethnography of Speaking. Richard Bauman and
    Joel Sherzer, eds. Cambridge University Press. pp. 283-308.

_____. 1975. "A parable in context: a social interactional analy-
    sis of storytelling performance." In Folklore: Performance and
    Communication. Dan Ben-Amos and Kenneth S. Goldstein, eds.
    Mouton and Co. The Hague. pp. 105-30.

_____. 1976a. "Bibliographic survey of the literature on speech
    play and related subjects." In Kirshenblatt-Gimblett, ed. 1976b
    pp. 179-223.

_____, ed. 1976b. Speech Play: Research and Resources for the
    Study of Linguistic Creativity. University of Pennsylvania Press
    Philadelphia.

Labov, William. 1970. "The study of language in its social context." Studium Generale 23: 30-87.

_____. 1971. "The notion of 'system' in creole languages." In Dell Hymes, ed. Pidginization and Creolization of Languages. Cambridge University Press. Cambridge. pp. 447-72.

_____. 1972a. Language in the Inner City: Studies in the Black English Vernacular. University of Pennsylvania Press. Philadelphia.

_____. 1972b. Sociolinguistic Patterns. University of Pennsylvania Press. Philadelphia.

Labov, William and David Fanshel. 1977. Therapeutic Discourse: psychotherapy as conversation. Academic Press. New York.

Landmann, Solcia. 1964. *Jiddisch: das Abenteuer einer Sprache*. Deutscher Taschenbuch Verlag. München.

Lavandera, Beatriz. 1978. "Where does the sociolinguistic variable stop?" Language in Society 7.2: 171-82.

Matisoff, James A. 1969. "Lahu bilingual humor." Acta Linguistica Hafniensia (Copenhagen) 12.2: 171-206.

_____. 1973. The Grammar of Lahu. University of California Publications in Linguistics, No. 75. University of California Press. Berkeley and Los Angeles.

_____. 1974. *"Sifrut ha-bituy b'Yidish: lashon psikho-ostensivit ba-dibur ha-amimi."* Complete Hebrew translation of 1973 version of Psycho-Ostensive Expressions in Yiddish, by Chana Kaufman Kronfeld. *Ha-sifrut* [Literature] No. 18-19, pp. 181-223. Tel Aviv. [A list of errata was printed in *Ha-sifrut* No. 21, p.168 (1975).]

_____. 1976. "Austro-Thai and Sino-Tibetan: an examination of body-part contact relationships." In Mantaro J. Hashimoto, ed. Genetic Relationship, Diffusion, and Typological Similarities of East and Southeast Asian Languages. Japan Society for the Promotion of Science. Tokyo. pp. 256-89.

_____. 1977. "Malediction and psycho-semantic theory: the case of Yiddish." Maledicta (The International Journal of Verbal Aggression) 1.1: 31-9.

_____. 1978a. <u>Variational Semantics in Tibeto-Burman: the "organ-ic" approach to linguistic comparison</u>. Institute for the Study of Human Issues. Philadelphia.

_____. 1978b. "Lahu religious poetry: a grammatical, cultural, and literary appreciation." Talk presented at Mekong River Festival, University of Hawaii (May, 1978).

_____. 1978c. "Linguistic diversity and language contact in Thailand." To appear in Wanat Bhruksasri and John McKinnon, eds., <u>Highlanders of Thailand</u>.

Montagu, M. F. 1967. <u>The Anatomy of Swearing</u>. Macmillan. New York.

Ochs, Eleanor, and Bambi B. Schieffelin, eds. [in press]. <u>Develop-mental Pragmatics</u>. Academic Press. New York.

Olson, David R. 1976. "From utterance to text: the bias of language in speech and writing." In H. Fisher and R. Diez-Gurerro, eds., <u>Language and Logic in Personality and Society</u>. New York.

Olsvanger, Immanuel. 1921. *Rosinkes mit Mandlen* [Raisins and Al-monds]. 2nd edition, 1931. Verlag der Schweizerischen Gesell-schaft für Volkskunde. Basle.

_____. 1935. *Reyte Pomeranzen* [Blood Oranges]. Schocken Verlag. Berlin.

_____. 1947. *Röyte Pomerantsen*: <u>Jewish Folk Humor</u>. First paper-back edition, 1965. Schocken Books. New York.

_____. 1949. *L'Chayim!* [To Life!]: <u>Jewish Wit and Humor</u>. Schocken Books. New York.

Ornstein, Robert. 1972. <u>The Psychology of Consciousness</u>. W. H. Freeman and Co. San Francisco.

Roback, Abraham A. 1933. <u>Curiosities of Yiddish Literature</u>. Sci-art Publishers. Cambridge, Mass.

_____. 1938. "Psychological aspects of Jewish protective phrases. <u>Bulletin of the Jewish Academy of Arts and Sciences</u>, No. 4. 16 pages. New York.

Rosten, Leo. 1968. <u>The Joys of Yiddish</u>. McGraw-Hill. New York.

Rovner, Ruth. 1977. "Oy! Look who's talking Yiddish." <u>Today Magazine</u>, October 2. Philadelphia.

Samuel, Maurice. 1971. In Praise of Yiddish. Cowles. New York.

Sankoff, David, ed. 1978. Linguistic Variation Models and Methods.
Academic Press. New York, San Francisco, London.

Saporta, Sol, ed. 1961. Psycholinguistics: a book of readings.
Holt, Rinehart, and Winston. New York.

Schaechter, Mordkhe. 1954. "On children's nonsense oaths in Yiddish."
In Uriel Weinreich, ed. The Field of Yiddish I. Linguistic Circle
of New York. New York. pp. 196-8.

_____. [to appear]. Yiddish Two: a textbook for intermediate
courses. [Preliminary edition (1976), sponsored by the Judah
Zelitch Foundation for a Living Yiddish and the Foundation for the
Advancement of Standard Yiddish. New York.].

Schegloff, Emanuel A. 1968. "Sequencing in conversational openings."
American Anthropologist 70.6: 1075-95.

Singer, Joe. 1977. How to Curse in Yiddish. (Entertain Your Friends!
Terrify Your Enemies!). Ballantine Books. New York.

Stutchkoff, Nahum. 1950. *Der Oytser fun der Yídisher Shprakh.* [The
Treasures of the Yiddish Language]. YIVO Institute for Jewish Research. New York.

Tannen, Deborah F. 1976. "Communication mix and mixup, or How linguistics can ruin a marriage." San Jose State Occasional Papers
in Linguistics. Dept. of Linguistics, San Jose State University.
San Jose, California. pp. 205-12.

_____. 1977. "Well, what did you expect?" In Kenneth Whistler,
et al., eds. Proceedings of the Third Annual Meeting of the
Berkeley Linguistics Society. Berkeley, California. pp. 506-15.

_____. [to appear, 1979]. "What's in a frame? Surface evidence
for underlying expectations." In Roy Freedle, ed. Discourse
Processing: New Directions. Ablex. Norwood, New Jersey.

Tannen, Deborah and Piyale Cömert Öztek. 1977. "Health to our mouths:
formulaic expressions in Turkish and Greek." In Kenneth Whistler,
et al., eds. Proceedings of the Third Annual Meeting of the
Berkeley Linguistics Society. Berkeley, California. pp. 516-34.

Telford, J. H.   1937.   "Animism in Kengtung State."   Journal of the
    Burma Research Society 27, part II: 85-238.

Tracy, Robert.   1965.   "Leopold Bloom fourfold: a Hungarian-Hebraic-
    Hellenic-Hibernian hero."   Massachusetts Review VI: 523-38.

Wald, Benji.   1976.   "The *Discourse Unit:* a study in the segmentation
    and form of spoken discourse."   MS.

Walker, Anthony R.   1970a.   Lahu Nyi (Red Lahu) Village Society and
    Economy in North Thailand.   mimeo MS.   Report submitted to the
    Tribal Research Centre, Chiang Mai University.   Chiang Mai,
    Thailand.

_____.   1970b.   "The Lahu Nyi (Red Lahu) New Year celebrations."
    Journal of the Siam Society 58, part I: 1-44.

Weinreich, Uriel.   1949.   College Yiddish: an Introduction to the
    Yiddish Language and to Jewish Life and Culture.   4th revised
    edition, 2nd printing, 1966.   YIVO Institute for Jewish Research.
    New York.

_____.   1953.   Languages in Contact.   Linguistic Circle of New York
    New York.

_____, ed.   1954.   The Field of Yiddish (I).   Linguistic Circle
    of New York.   New York.

_____, ed.   1965.   The Field of Yiddish (II).   Mouton and Company.
    The Hague.

_____.   1968.   Modern English-Yiddish Yiddish-English Dictionary.
    YIVO Institute for Jewish Research and McGraw-Hill.   New York.

Yídishe Shprakh: a Journal devoted to the problems of standard Yiddish
    [from January - February, 1941].   YIVO Institute for Jewish Re-
    search.   New York.

Zaretski, A.   1929.   *Yídishe Gramatik.*   [Yiddish Grammar].   Revised
    edition.   Vilner Farlag fun B. Kletskin.   Vilna.

Zimmer, Karl E.   1958.   "Situational formulas: a cultural-linguistic
    phenomenon."   MS.   [University of Michigan (Anthropology 116)
    term paper].

2 3 4 5 6 7 8 9 10 11 12 13   88 87 86 85 84 83 82 81 80